Creative Kids
Complete Photo Guide to

Knitting

First published in the United States of America by
Creative Publishing international, a division of
Quarto Publishing Group USA Inc.
400 First Avenue North
Suite 400
Minneapolis, MN 55401
1-800-328-3895
www.creativepub.com
Visit www.Craftside.net for a behind-the-scenes peek at our crafty world!

ISBN: 978-1-58923-869-5

Digital edition published in 2015
eISBN: 978-1-62788-255-2
10 9 8 7 6 5 4 3 2 1

Library of Congress Cataloging-in-Publication Data
available

Technical Editor: Karen Frisa
Copy Editor: Karen Levy
Design and Layout: Laura McFadden Design, Inc.
Illustrations of Kids: iStock
Technical Illustrations: Karen Frisa
Photographs: Patrick F. Smith
Printed in China

Creative Kids

Complete
Photo Guide to
Knitting

Mary Scott Huff

Creative Publishing
international

contents

For my parents, who taught me how to speak, and my children,
who taught me how to listen.

Introduction

"A knitter only appears to be knitting yarn. Also being knitted are winks, mischief, sighs, fragrant possibilities, wild dreams."
—**Dr. SunWolf**

The art of knitting predates the written word. So while a book about how to do it will be helpful for modern learners, it's not the whole story. The very best way to learn knitting is to do it together with friends and loved ones.

If you are an adult, either teaching or learning together with a child, this volume will take you step by step through the basics, and then beyond. If you are a child, either teaching or learning together with an adult, the process should be much the same.

In either case, using this book is simple and intuitive. You can choose to read through the process in the technique chapters and practice each step. Or you can pick a project you like, and follow the steps for making it. Each pattern will direct you to the information you need.

In addition to projects and techniques, yarn and knitted fabric, the pages that follow will tell you about tools that make knitting easier and more fun, and a few of the many great ways to connect with other knitters.

It is my great privilege to introduce new knitters of all ages to the delights that await you in the world of yarn and needles. The best thing about knitting is the people who do it. Welcome, and thank you for joining us!

I invite you to sit side by side, hold each other's yarn, and discover the magic of playing with string. Together.

"Now, let us all take a deep breath and forge on into the future; knitting at the ready."—**Elizabeth Zimmermann**

Knitting Mechanics

In order to knit, you only need needles, yarn, and persistence. The actual act of making stitches requires only two skills: knitting, and purling. Once you master these two stitches, there's nothing you can't knit, because everything you do will be some variation of the knit and the purl.

No matter what type of project you choose to knit, you'll use these three steps: casting on, knitting (and/or purling), and binding off.

Cast On

In order to start knitting, you'll need to get a foundation row of stitches onto your needles. This is called casting on. There are many different ways to cast on, but we'll start with two: the cable cast on and the long-tail cast on. Almost every kind of cast on begins with a slipknot.

Slipknot

1 Make a loop in the end of your yarn, about 6" (13 cm) from the end.

2 Put your two fingers through the loop.

3 Grasp the strand (the one coming from the yarn ball, not the tail).

4 Pull the strand through the loop.

5 Pull the loop to tighten the knot around it.

6 Place the slipknot on your needle. Pull on the working strand to snug the slipknot up to the needle.

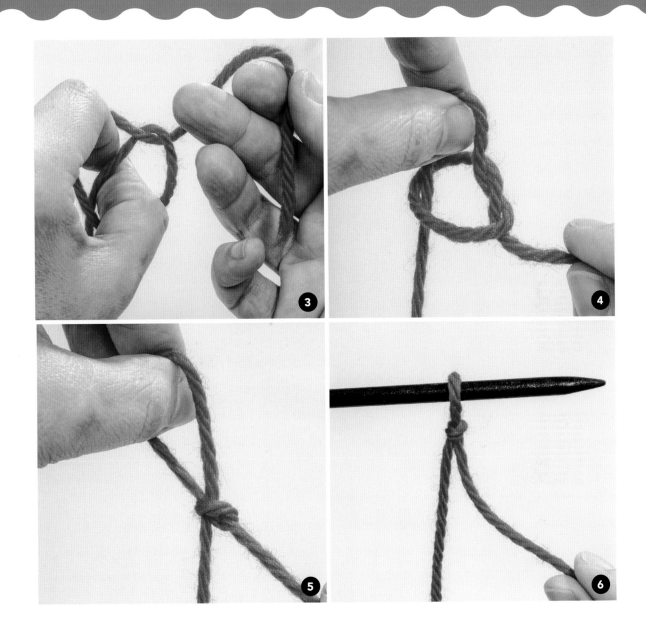

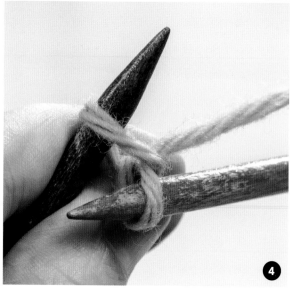

Cable Cast On

The cable cast on is named for the way its lower edge looks when complete—kind of like a twisted rope or cable. Here are the steps to do it:

1 Make a slipknot and place it on your needle.

2 Holding the needle with the slipknot in your left hand, place the point of the right needle through it, from front to back.

3 Wrap the yarn around and between the two needles, from back to front.

4 Use the point of the right needle to pull the strand through.

5 Without taking the slipknot off the left needle, pull the new stitch up and over onto the left needle.

6 For the next and all subsequent stitches, put the tip of the right needle between the last two stitches.

7 Repeat steps 3 through 6 until you have cast on all the stitches you need.

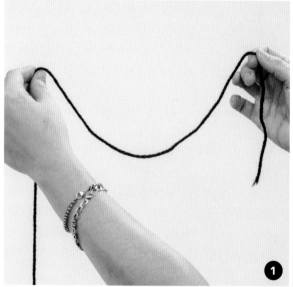 

Long-Tail Cast On

The long-tail cast on uses only one needle and two strands of yarn to make each stitch. One strand comes from the yarn ball, and the other strand is a long tail.

1 Allowing about ½" (1 cm) for each stitch you plan to cast on, measure from the end of the yarn strand to your starting point.

2 Make a slipknot and place it on your needle.

3 Holding the needle in your right hand, place the two fingers of your left hand between the hanging strands.

4 Spread the fingers apart and lower the needle so that the yarn makes a V between the thumb and forefinger. Use the forefinger of your right hand to hold the slipknot on the needle.

5 Pass the needle under the thumb strand.

6 Pass the needle over the forefinger strand.

7 Draw the thumb out from the yarn loop and tug lightly on the yarn tails to tighten the stitch.

8 Repeat steps 3 through 7 until you have cast on all the stitches you need.

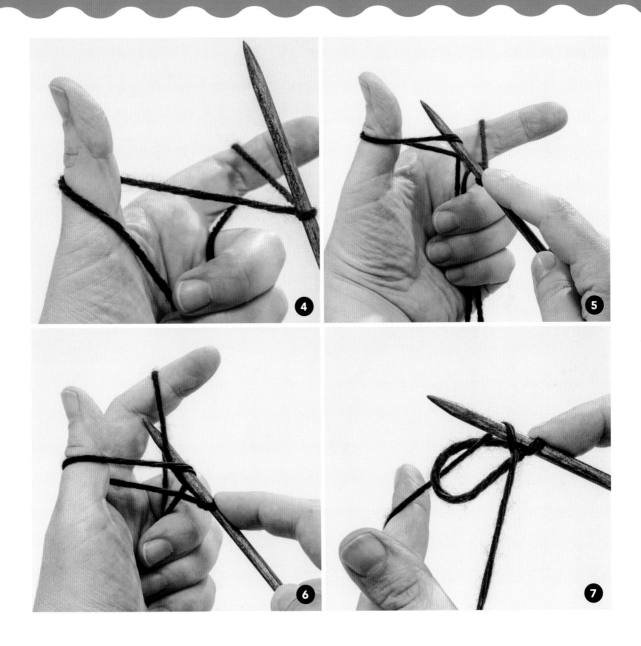

Knit

Once you have completed a row of cast-on stitches, you're ready to knit them. Here's how:

1. Hold the needle with the stitches to be worked in your left hand.

2. Put the right needle through the stitch, front to back.

3. Wrap the yarn around and between the needles, back to front.

4. Use the right needle to pull the strand through.

5. Let the old stitch come off the end of the left needle.

6. Repeat steps 2 through 5 until all the stitches from the left needle have been knitted onto the right needle. That's one row of knitting complete!

   To knit another row, turn the needle with the stitches on it around so its point faces to the right. This is known as "turning the work." Now hold it with your left hand and switch the empty needle to your right hand. Knit the next row. Fabric made by knitting every stitch of every row is known as "garter stitch."

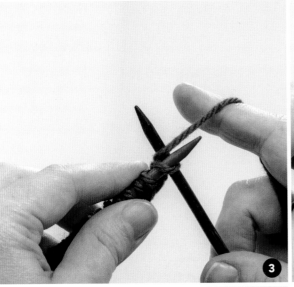

tip Especially when you are just starting out, try not to stop knitting until the entire row is complete. If you stop in the middle of the row, it can be hard to tell which direction you were going when you come back to knitting. If it can't be helped, try to remember which color needle was in each hand for when you come back.

Here's a rhyme to help you remember the steps for each knitted stitch:

In through the front door (step 2)
Around the back (step 3)
Out through the window (step 4)
And off jumps Jack (step 5)

Purl

Working a purl stitch is almost the same as working a knit stitch, with two important differences: 1. When purling, the working strand is held in front of the work, rather than in back, as in knitting. 2. When purling, the right needle goes into the stitch from back to front, rather than from front to back, as in knitting.

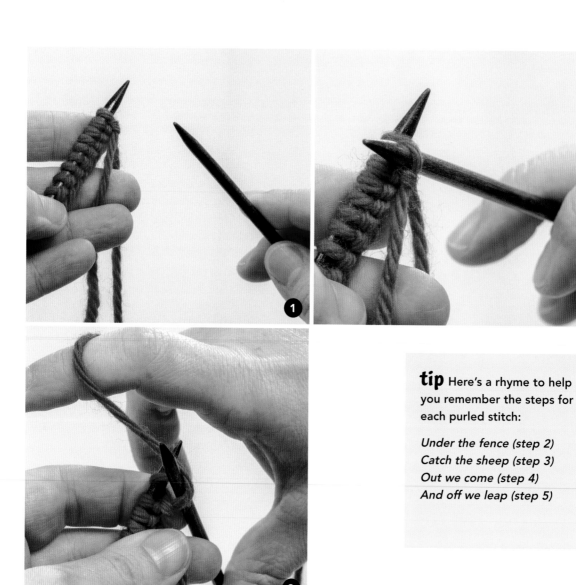

tip Here's a rhyme to help you remember the steps for each purled stitch:

Under the fence (step 2)
Catch the sheep (step 3)
Out we come (step 4)
And off we leap (step 5)

1   Hold the needle with the stitches to be worked in your left hand.

2   Put the right needle through the stitch, back to front.

3   Wrap the yarn around and between the needles, back to front.

4   Use the right needle to pull the strand through.

5   Let the old stitch come off the end of the left needle.

6   Repeat steps 2 through 5 until all the stitches from the left needle have been purled onto the right needle. That's one row of purling complete!

To purl another row, turn the needle with the stitches on it around so its point faces to the right. This is known as "turning the work." Now hold it in your left hand and switch the empty needle to your right hand. Purl the next row. Fabric made by purling every stitch of every row is known as "garter stitch."

If you knit one row, turn the work, and then purl the next row, you'll be working in "stockinette stitch," possibly the most common form of knitting. Try working alternating knit and purl rows a few times, to see how stockinette stitch (St st) is different from garter stitch.

Practice knitting complete rows, then purling complete rows, counting your stitches to make sure you have the same number you cast on. Keep practicing until you can work whole rows without any mistakes, dropped or added stitches. Once you're good at doing complete rows, practice switching between knit stitches and purl stitches, remembering to move the working yarn to the back between stitches for knitting, and to the front between stitches for purling.

Bind Off

At the end of your knitting, you create a finished upper edge that won't unravel, by binding off. Knitted stitches should be bound off knitwise, and purled stitches should be bound off purlwise. This is known as binding off in pattern.

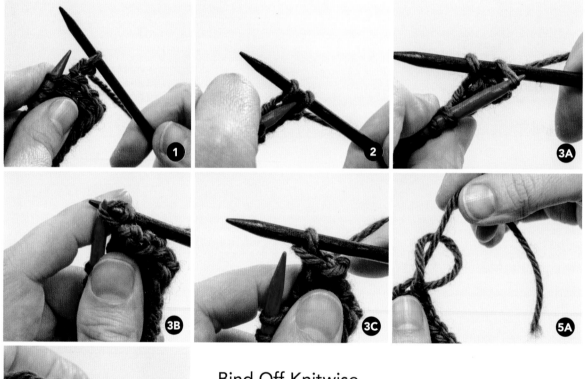

Bind Off Knitwise

To bind off knitwise, follow these steps:

1 Knit one stitch.

2 Knit another stitch.

3 Use the tip of the left needle to pass the first stitch over the last one.

4 Repeat steps 2 and 3 until all the stitches from the left needle are bound off, and only the last stitch remains on the right needle.

5 Break the yarn, leaving a tail of about 6" (13 cm). Pass the tail through the last stitch and pull gently to tighten.

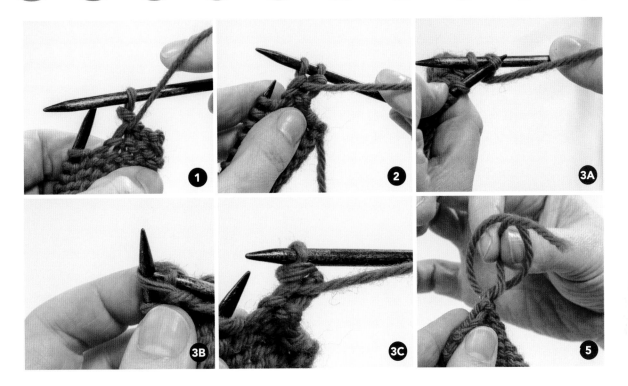

Bind Off Purlwise

To bind off purlwise, follow these steps:

1 Purl one stitch.

2 Purl another stitch.

3 Use the tip of the left needle to pass the first stitch over the last one.

4 Repeat steps 2 and 3 until all the stitches from the left needle are bound off, and only the last stitch remains on the right needle.

5 Break the yarn, leaving a tail of about 6" (13 cm). Pass the tail through the last stitch and pull gently to tighten.

Casting on, knitting, purling, and binding off are the most important skills in knitting. Take your time and have patience as you practice, remembering that mistakes are part of the process of learning. Here are a few more skills that will help you as you practice knitting and purling: frogging, tinking, and retrieving a dropped stitch.

Frogging

Knitters say that they "frog" their knitting when a big mistake happens and they "rip-it, rip-it." In other words, sometimes the best and fastest way to undo a mistake is to remove the needles from the knitting and pull on the working strand until the entire piece unravels. You can also frog just a few rows of knitting, say, back to just before the mistake, then put the needles carefully back into the live stitch loops. Don't be afraid to pull out mistakes; even the most experienced knitters do it all the time. Think of frogging as a great big eraser for your knitting mistakes. You'll only do it better the next time!

Tinking

Knit spelled backward is tink, and to tink means to "un-knit." When you notice a mistake made just a few stitches back, there's no need to remove the needles and rip out a lot of knitting. To tink, first turn the work so the newest stitches are on the left and the working yarn is coming from the left needle. Then, place the tip of your right needle into the stitch below the mistake, and pull gently on the working strand to unravel one stitch. Do this stitch by stitch, until you get back to the mistake, then fix it and continue on.

Retrieve a Dropped Stitch

When a stitch has accidentally fallen off the needle without being worked, it's said to have "dropped." You can tell this has happened when you count fewer stitches than you know you should have on your needle, and you can see where a "ladder" of stitches has formed in your fabric. Don't worry; you can pick up a dropped stitch again without having to frog your knitting. You'll need a crochet hook to do it most easily.

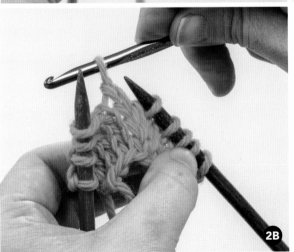

1 Locate the dropped stitch, and work up to where it should be on the needle.

2 Put the crochet hook into the loop of the dropped stitch, from front to back. Use the hook to pick up the next "ladder rung" above the stitch, then the next, and so on, until all the ladder rungs have been looped through one another. Check the back of your work to make sure you haven't skipped any rungs. Place the last rung on your left knitting needle, and continue knitting.

Shaping Your Knitting

Once you have confidence in knitting flat fabric, you're ready to learn how to create shaping. In order to shape knitting, we either add or subtract stitches according to the pattern directions. Adding stitches is known as increasing, while subtracting stitches is known as decreasing. Here are a couple of different ways for doing each.

Increases

Kfb (knit into the front and back)

When pattern instructions call for you to "kfb," you'll make two stitches from one.

Knit into the stitch as you normally would, but don't slip it off the left needle yet.

Pivot your work toward you so that you can see the back leg of the stitch you just knitted into, then knit into it, too.

Let the original stitch slip off the left needle. You now have two stitches where there was one.

YO (yarn over)

When pattern instructions call for you to "yo," you'll make a new stitch by laying the working yarn over the top of the right needle between two stitches.

Knit to the point where the pattern instructs you to make a yarnover.

Bring the yarn to the front of the work between two stitches, then over the top of the right needle, and to the back again.

Continue knitting. The yo increase creates a hole in the knitting where the new stitch has formed.

Decreases

K2tog (knit two together)

When pattern instructions call for you to "k2tog," you'll eliminate one stitch by creating a decrease that leans to the right.

1 Work to the point where the pattern instructs you to k2tog, then put the tip of the right needle through the next two stitches at the same time.

2 Wrap the yarn as you normally would to knit.

3 Pull one new stitch through the two old ones.

4 Let the two stitches slip off the left needle. Continue knitting. You now have one stitch where there were two (arrow).

SSK (slip, slip, knit)

When pattern instructions call for you "SSK," you'll eliminate one stitch by creating a decrease that leans to the left.

1 Work to the point where the pattern instructs you to SSK, then slip one stitch to the right needle as if to knit it (knitwise).

2 Slip the next stitch to the right needle as if to knit it (knitwise).

3 Put the tip of the left needle into the fronts of the two stitches you just slipped.

4 Wrap the yarn and pull a new stitch through the two old ones, letting them slip off the left needle.

Knit in the Round

Now that you understand the basics of flat knitting, it's time to try circular knitting, or knitting in the round. Worked with circular (circ) or double-pointed needles (DPN), knitting in the round creates cylindrical, tubular shapes, with no side edges. The diameter of the tube you knit is determined by the number of stitches you cast on. Short circular needles and double-pointed needles are used for smaller tubes (such as hats or sleeves), while longer circular needles are for larger tubes (like sweater bodies).

Join a Round

1 To begin knitting in the round, cast on as usual, using a circular needle. To start out, use a 16" (40.5 cm) long circular needle in a size appropriate for your yarn. Once you have cast on all the stitches you need, add one more, extra stitch.

2 Lay your needle on a table with the tips pointed toward one another to make a circle. Keeping the needle as flat against the table as you can, twist the cast-on stitches so that the tops of the stitches (the loops) are all on the outside of the circle, and the bottoms of the stitches (the knots) are all on the inside of the circle.

3 Keeping the stitches arranged properly, carefully pick up the needles. Slip the first stitch on the right needle over to the left needle, where the tail is. Now knit the first two stitches on the left needle together (k2tog) to join the round.

Mark and Keep Track of Rounds

Once you knit an entire circle of stitches, you'll be back to the point where you joined the round. Place a marker (PM) between the last and the first stitch of the round.

From this point forward, if you knit every stitch, the fabric you get will be stockinette stitch, even though you never purled. This is the magic of circular knitting: there are no wrong side rows when you knit spiral tubes. Count the rows or measure the length of your piece only when you reach the marker, so you can be sure you've completely finished each round of knitting.

Yarn and Knitted Fabric

The most important decision you make about each of your knitted projects will be which yarn to use. Knitting designers help you make your decisions by telling you specifically which yarn they used to create the original sample. If you use the same identical yarn, the decision is easy. But what if you need to choose something else? Using a yarn other than that specified by your pattern is known as "yarn substitution," and knitters make substitutions all the time. In order to choose a yarn that will give the desired result, there are a few things to consider.

Weight

The first characteristic to compare between the specified yarn and your substitution is its weight. Generally speaking, the heavier the weight, the larger needle you'll use, resulting in fewer and larger stitches in each 1" (2.5 cm) of knitted fabric.

New yarn is labeled with information about how thick it is, known as its "symbol." The larger the number in the symbol, the thicker the yarn. Choose a yarn with the same symbol as the one used in your pattern. Selecting a heavier or lighter yarn symbol will result in a larger or smaller finished item.

Gauge

Another important consideration for the yarn you choose will be its suggested gauge. This is also specified on the label, with a symbol like the one shown here.

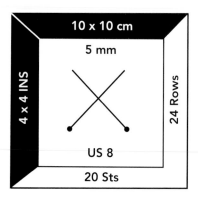

Gauge is always measured like this: Imagine a square of stockinette stitch knitting that is exactly 4" (10 cm) square. The gauge symbol is a simple drawing of that square. The needle drawing tells you what size needle the manufacturer suggests you use. The numbers specify how many stitches and how many rows will be in the square, when knitted with that size needle. In the example above, a 4" (10 cm) square of stockinette stitch knitting will contain 20 stitches per row and 24 rows, if you knit it with a size US 8 (5 mm) needle. It's important to choose yarn that fits the same gauge as that specified in your pattern, in order to get a finished project of the right size. Even after checking the gauge information, you'll still need to complete a gauge swatch of your own before beginning your project to make sure the needles you choose create the fabric you need. See page 36 for more information on swatching.

Fiber

The next thing to think about is the fiber your yarn is made of. Different yarns are made from different fibers, or blends of fibers. Generally, fiber can be divided into three different categories: natural, manmade, and blends.

Natural fibers come either from the trimmed coats of animals or from plants. Wool, cashmere, silk, and alpaca are all examples of natural fibers derived from animals. Cotton, linen, and hemp all originate from plants.

Manmade fibers are derived from chemical mixtures made in textile factories. Examples of manmade fibers are acrylic, polyester, nylon, and rayon.

Blends are combinations of different fibers in varying amounts, trying to provide the best parts of each. Blended fibers can be made from any combination of natural and manmade fibers.

Besides the way each yarn feels, the most important consideration in choosing the fiber for your project will be how you care for it. Some fibers are machine washable and dryable, while others aren't. Some are delicate and require special care, while others are durable and hardwearing. Think about how your project will be cared for (and by whom!) as you consider the choices.

Ply and Twist

Another component of the yarn you choose will be its construction. These are known as its ply and twist. The number of plies (strands) and the tightness or looseness of the twist can affect the way your knitted stitches look.

Fibers are held together in strands by twisting them together. The act of creating strands by twisting them is known as "spinning." Spinning can be done by hand, using a spindle or a spinning wheel, or by machine, in a textile mill. The tightness or looseness of the twist in each strand can influence its strength as well as the way the finished yarn looks and behaves.

The individual strands of fiber in a yarn are known as "plies." Yarns that have only one ply are known as "single-ply." Yarns with more than one ply are named after the number of plies they contain, such as "two-ply," "three-ply," and so on. Not all yarns specify the number of plies they have, but you can easily tell for yourself by separating the strands at the cut end of a yarn strand.

Blocking

One last important characteristic of yarn is how the knitted fabric will look and measure after it has been washed and dried as the manufacturer suggests.

Imagine how your shirt looks when you take it out of the dryer: sometimes it needs to be hung up for a while, or even pressed with an iron to look its very best. Knitting is somewhat the same. Once the knitting is all done, the project usually needs to be wetted and dried, or even steamed, to look really finished. This final touch is known as "blocking," and sometimes it can affect the end gauge of your knitting. The best way to know whether a yarn you're considering will be a good substitute is to make a gauge swatch, and then block it as the manufacturer suggests. Only then can you be sure you've chosen a winner.

Swatching

The act of making a small piece of "practice" knitting before you start your project is known as swatching. There are lots of reasons why you might want to create swatches.

tip If your first swatch isn't quite right, don't frog it. Bind it off and attach a tag with the needle size you used and the number of stitches and rows you got. "Wrong" swatches are still useful for testing different blocking techniques.

Determine the Best Needle Size

The information on your yarn's label (see page 33) gives you a starting point for what size needles to use for your project. But every knitter and every yarn is different, so you can never assume that your yarn and needles will give you the exact same number of stitches and rows that the manufacturer suggests or the designer used for your pattern, even when you use the exact same yarn and needles as the designer chose. This becomes really important when you are trying to make a garment or an accessory in a particular size. If your gauge is smaller or larger than it should be, your finished project will be smaller or larger than you want. The solution is to do a little experimental knitting first, using different sizes of needles with the same number of stitches and the same yarn.

Practice Stitch Patterns

In addition to achieving the correct gauge, swatching is useful for getting to know your yarn. Once you know which needle is right, practice the stitch patterns called for in your pattern, to get a feel for how they look in your yarn and how it feels to work them. With practice, you'll be able to learn from swatching whether your yarn works better with wood or metal needles, sharp or blunt points, and firm or loose tension. Take your time and have fun experimenting.

Make a Swatch

With the size needles suggested in your pattern (remember, this may be different from what the manufacturer suggests, depending on the effect the designer wanted to achieve), cast on the number of stitches listed under "gauge." Knit in stockinette stitch (alternating knit and purl rows) until the swatch measures 4" (10 cm) long from the beginning. If your swatch has the same number of rows and is the same width (4" or 10 cm) as stated in your pattern, then you're all set: you have achieved the correct gauge. If your swatch has fewer rows than the pattern's gauge or is wider than 4" (10 cm), then try again with smaller needles. If your swatch has more rows than the pattern's gauge or is narrower than 4" (10 cm), then try again with larger needles. Be patient and keep trying with different needles until you get the gauge you need.

Try Out Blocking Techniques

If you have more than one swatch, you can try different ways of blocking. Referring to page 52 and 53, block each swatch with a different technique. This is the best way to decide what kind of blocking makes your knitting look best, without worrying that you'll accidentally damage your finished project. Even if you only try one technique on one swatch, you'll be more confident when you do your final blocking.

How to Measure

Knitting instructions will most often tell you to knit until each piece reaches a certain length, rather than a particular number of rows. This is because even when you knit exactly to the same gauge, there can still be subtle differences in how many rows you get in the same length of knitting. To get accurate results, follow the same steps every time you measure, and for every piece.

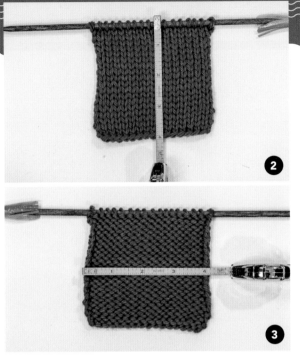

1 **LAY THE KNITTING FLAT.**
Put it on a hard floor or table, rather than a carpeted or upholstered surface, and never measure your knitting in your lap. This is because any surface that yields to pressure (like a pillow) can give inconsistent measurements.

2 Using your retractable tape measure (see "Measuring Tools," page 134), hook the end over the top of your needle, and measure down to the bottom edge of the piece.

3 Some stitch patterns are more challenging to measure than others. Stockinette stitch, for example, is notoriously tricky because its edges curl in. To measure the width of a piece, try laying it wrong side up (with the purl side facing you). Place your tape measure from side to side in the middle of the piece to check its width.

How to Count Stitches and Rows

When working on gauge swatches, you'll be counting the number of stitches and rows in a 4" (10 cm) area. Counting them accurately is the only way to know whether you've obtained the gauge or not.

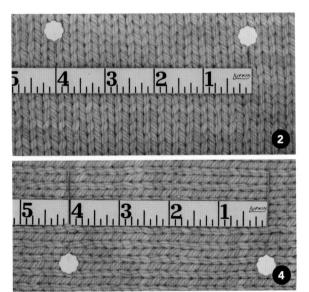

1 Lay the knitting flat as you did for taking measurements.

2 Find the exact edge of a knitted stitch, and put a pin in it. With a 6" (15 cm) ruler (see "Measuring Tools," page 134), find the exact edge of a stitch in the same row, exactly 4" (10 cm) away, and put a second pin in it.

3 Leaving the ruler in place, carefully count all the stitches between pins. Pointing a knitting needle at each stitch and counting out loud can help with this step.

4 Now count the rows in 4" (10 cm) the same way (the stitches on your needle count as a row, too).

Special Techniques

In addition to the basic skills in the previous chapter, the projects in this book call for some other specific procedures. This chapter is the place to learn about them.

Wind a Ball from a Skein

Some yarn comes from the mill already wound into a ball. In this case, it's easy to find an end (either on the outside of the ball or pulled from the center) and start knitting. Other yarn is sold in skeins, which need to be wound into balls before you can knit from them.

1 Remove the label from your skein and save it for future reference (care instructions, gauge, etc.).

2 Carefully untwist the skein so it forms a big loop of many strands, and locate the knot. These are the two ends of the skein. Untie or cut the knot off with scissors, and carefully work the two ends loose from the loop of strands.

3 Have a helper hold the skein open with two hands. Take one of the two free ends from the knot and wind it around two of your fingers.

4 After eight or ten wraps around your fingers, take the yarn off. Twist it like a figure eight and fold it in half.

5 Wind the rest of the skein around this mini-ball. Important: Don't wind the yarn tightly! This will stretch the yarn, which could ruin your project. The ball should be as loose as possible while still holding together.

Join a New Strand

When one ball of yarn runs out, you'll need to join another one to it in order to continue. You'll also need to join a new strand to an old one when changing colors. Here are two ways to do it.

Overhand Knot

Holding both strands together, form a loop.

Put both ends through the loop and pull to tighten, making sure the knot is as close to the knitting as possible.

Weaver's Knot

Make a slipknot in strand.

Put the end of strand 2 through the slipknot.

Pull the two tails of strand 1 apart (A) until strand 2 pops through the center of the slipknot (B).

Slip a Stitch

When slipping a stitch, you simply move it from the left needle to the right, as if to purl, without actually working it.

Put the tip of the right needle into the stitch, from back to front (as if to purl).

Slip the stitch from the left needle onto the right, without making a new stitch.

Join Knitted Pieces

Sometimes we knit separate pieces and then join them together. Other times, we start knitting from the edge of a previously knitted piece instead of casting on. Here are some ways to do both.

Mattress Stitch

1 With right sides up, place two edges to be joined side by side, matching the top and bottom. If the seam is very long, use opening stitch markers (see Knitting Tools, page 135) to hold the edges together every few inches.

2 Thread a tapestry needle with a length of matching yarn, about twice as long as your seam (we're using contrasting yarn here, so you can see it better).

3 Sew under the bar of each knitted stitch, first on one side of the seam, then on the other, without pulling the stitches all the way tight.

4 After making six or so stitches, pull them snug, joining the edges. Pull tightly enough to make your sewn stitches disappear, but not so tightly that the seam puckers.

5 Repeat steps 3 and 4 to the end of the seam, then fasten the sewing yarn. Weave both ends back into the seam and trim closely.

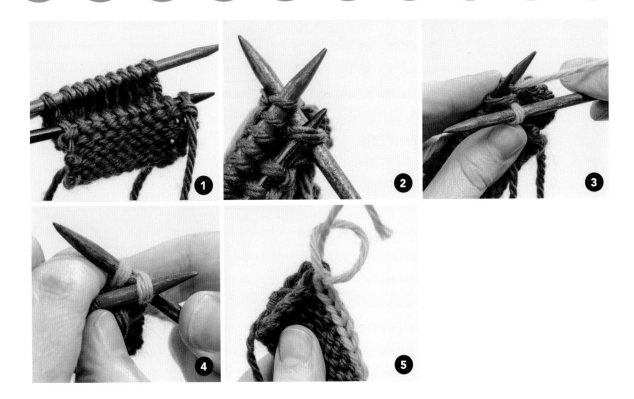

Three-Needle Bind Off

This is a great way to join two pieces of knitting (or two edges of the same piece), without any sewing.

1 Place circular or double-pointed needles into the stitches of the two edges to be joined, and hold with right sides together in your left hand.

2 With your right hand, place the tip of a third needle into the first stitch on each holder.

3 Wrap the yarn and knit, pulling one new stitch through the two old ones, and slipping each old stitch off its holder.

4 Repeat steps 2 and 3. Pass the first stitch on your right needle over the second to bind off.

5 Break yarn and pull through last stitch, then weave in the end.

Pick Up and Knit

This technique is commonly used at neckline edges where ribbed trim will be added. Sometimes you pick up and knit along a top edge (through stitches), and sometimes you pick up and knit along a side edge (through rows). The picking up operation is the same, but how often you do it changes.

ALONG A TOP EDGE (THROUGH STITCHES):

1 Hold the knitted edge in your left hand, with the right side of the knitted fabric facing you.

2 Using the color indicated in your pattern (we're using a contrasting color here), put the tip of your right needle down through the first knitted stitch and pick up a loop of working yarn onto the right needle.

3 Continue picking up and knitting through every single knitted stitch on the edge.

Along a side edge (through rows):

1 Work steps 1 and 2 as for a top edge, but only repeat them through three knitted rows.

2 Skip the fourth knitted row, picking up the next three.

3 Continue picking up and knitting through three out of four knitted rows, until the desired number of stitches is on the right needle.

Weave Ends

When you finish knitting, there will be yarn strands left over at the beginning and end of the piece, and sometimes in the middle, if you joined other colors or balls of yarn. To make the piece tidy, you just need to weave them in (we're using contrasting yarn here, so you can see it better).

1. To weave in cast-on and bind-off tails, thread the end of the yarn tail through a tapestry needle (see "Knitting Tools," page 135).

2. Make stitches with the yarn tail through the edge of the knitting.

3. When the yarn tails are in the center of the piece, make stitches that follow the shape of the knitting.

4. Trim the yarn tail close to the knitting, being careful not to accidentally snip your knitted fabric. The weaving will be nearly invisible from the right side.

Knitted Cord

When you knit a small number of stitches without ever turning the work, a narrow tube will form, known as knitted cord.

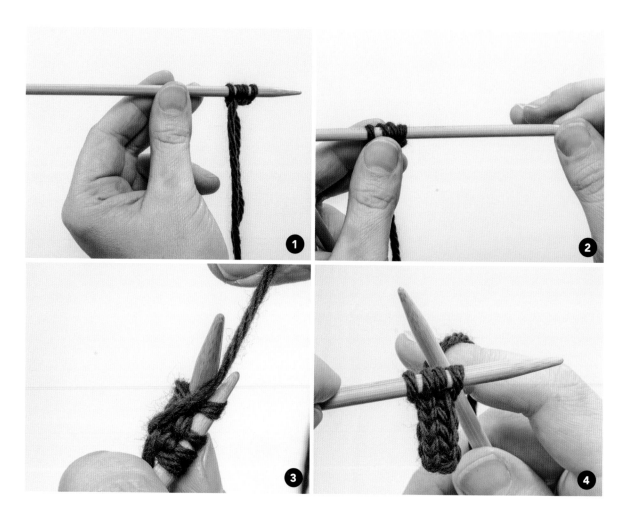

1 Using two double-pointed needles, or a short circular needle, cast on the required number of stitches, usually between 3 and 6. In this example we'll use 4.

2 Knit 4, then slide all the stitches to the other end of the needle.

3 Without turning the work, pull the working yarn across the back of all the stitches, and knit 4 again, giving the working yarn an extra tug after the first stitch.

4 Repeat steps 2 and 3 until the cord reaches the desired length.

Buttonhole

Although there are many ways to make buttonholes, this technique is perhaps the easiest.

1 Work to the specified point in your knitting instructions, then knit 2 stitches together (k2tog).

2 Make a yarnover right next to the k2tog decrease.

3 Continue working as directed. When you come to the loopy yarn-over stitch on the next row, work it as if it were a regular stitch. It will create a hole in the knitted fabric for the button to pass through.

Blocking

To look its best, most knitted fabric needs some sort of finishing. Depending on the fiber it's made from, your yarn will need some combination of moisture, heat, and manipulation to lie flat and even up the stitches. Finishing your knitted fabric is referred to as blocking. Here are a few ways to block your knitting.

Steaming

Place your knitting flat on an ironing board and use the steam from an iron to gently moisten and warm it. Leave it on the ironing board to dry, with pins to hold it in shape, if needed. When steaming your knitting, be careful not to touch the iron to the knitted fabric; hold it 2" to 3" (5 to 7.6 cm) away at all times. And of course, never touch the sole plate of the iron, or put your hand in the way of the steam.

tip Safety first! If you are under ten, have an adult handle the iron for you. If you are over ten, get an adult to supervise you when handling an iron.

Washing

Fill a basin with warm (not hot) water and add a small amount of wool wash (page 136). Add your knitting to the bath, gently pressing to remove all the air bubbles. Let it soak for at least 20 minutes. Gently squeeze the water out, without twisting or wringing. Lay the piece flat to dry, reshaping to the blocking measurements in your pattern's schematic (page 66) ,if necessary. If your finished piece has straight edges, be sure to straighten them by pinning them down to a carpeted floor, an ironing board, or a blocking mat (page 136) while it's still damp. Make sure your knitting has dried completely before proceeding.

Misting

Lay your knitting on a moisture-safe surface, such as a towel or blocking mat. Mist it with a spray bottle until the surface is damp, but not soaking wet. Straighten and shape the piece, using pins and consulting your pattern's schematics for measurements, if needed.

To choose the best blocking technique for your project, pay close attention to the care instructions provided on your yarn label. However they instruct you to care for the finished garment, that's a safe way for how to block your piece. For example, if your yarn's care instructions say "Hand wash in warm water, lay flat to dry," then that's probably a good method to block your knitting, too.

Felting

Some of the projects in this book call for you to knit them in a larger-than-usual size and then felt them. Felted knit fabric is much stiffer and more substantial than regular knitting.

There are several ways to felt your knitting, but they all require the same basic elements: water, heat, and agitation. Some pieces, like swatches and small details, are easier to felt by hand. Others are more manageable using a washing machine, due to their size or the yarn you're using. Every yarn will felt differently, so take your time and check on your progress as often as is practical. Remember: Only untreated (non-superwash) 100% animal fibers will felt. If other manmade fibers are added to the mix, your project will not felt, so check your labels carefully, and if in doubt, get the exact same yarn specified in the pattern.

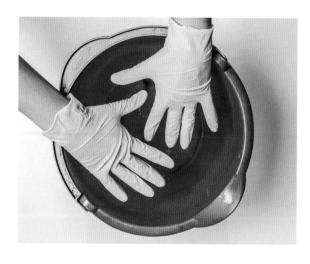

By Hand

Fill a bucket, sink, or bathtub with enough piping hot water to cover your piece, with room to swish it around aggressively. Add a squirt of dishwashing liquid or laundry detergent to remove any residual spinning oils and dirt from the yarn. Wearing rubber gloves will protect your hands as well as provide a little extra traction against the project, particularly if they have textured ridges on the palms. Add your project to the felting bath and let it sit for 20 or 30 minutes to allow the water to penetrate the fibers; this makes the felting go much more quickly. Then scrub, squish, smash, and generally throttle it in the hot water. The length of time you will need to continue this part varies greatly with each yarn type, so check your progress often by squeezing the water out of the piece and evaluating the fabric. Experiment with household utensils, like potato mashers, rubber plungers, and the like, particularly if your hands get tired. Add more hot water and detergent when the bath starts to cool. You can also give your project a "shock" rinse in cold water between baths to further the process.

By Machine

You may have heard that it is not possible to felt your knitting in a front-loading washing machine. While top-loading machines are generally faster, rest assured that they aren't the only way. Front loaders are gentler, and so may take longer, but they will get the job done. To begin, choose the hottest, shortest cycle on your machine. You may need to repeat the cycle, or choose a longer one, but it's safer to work in stages to avoid over-felting.

Place your project into a mesh laundry bag. This is to protect your machine from choking on loose fibers, should the yarn shed too much, and also to keep any small parts from getting lost. Add a pair of jeans or two, and a few clean tennis balls. Washable athletic shoes are also great for felting, particularly if they have rough soles; just be sure to remove the laces first. Use regular laundry detergent, but don't add liquid fabric softener. Start the machine and let the magic begin. After the machine has filled with water, stop the cycle and let the project sit for 20 or 30 minutes to allow the water to penetrate the fibers; this makes the felting go much more quickly. After resuming the cycle, check your project from time to time, if your washer allows (it's hard to stop a front-loader mid-cycle), to evaluate the felting.

Whether you felt by hand or by machine, you'll be able to tell the felting is complete when your piece matches the finished dimensions indicated in the pattern (or a bit smaller—you can always stretch felted items somewhat, but if they're too big, you can only do more felting). Generally speaking, the knitted stitches should no longer be defined, the surface of the fabric should have a fuzzy "halo," and the fabric should be smooth and even when you are done. If any of these properties is absent, but the size is correct, stop felting. If all these characteristics are present but the piece is still too large, felt some more.

Pompoms

Pompoms are just bundles of yarn that are tied tightly in the middle and trimmed evenly all around. Here are two ways to make them.

5B

Cardboard

1. Cut a piece of scrap cardboard to the size you'd like your pompom to be, if it were measured from its center out to the end of one yarn strand (for example, 1" [2.5 cm]). The length of the cardboard doesn't matter, only the width.

2. Cut a piece of yarn about 10" (25 cm) long and thread it through a tapestry needle. Place it nearby so you'll have it ready for step 4.

3. Wrap your yarn around the cardboard as many times as you think will make a nice fluffy pompom. There's no right or wrong number of wraps, but it usually takes more wrapping than you might think. If you want to make several pompoms all the same, take note of the number of wraps you made.

4. Cut the yarn and hold it to the cardboard so it won't unwrap. Get your threaded tapestry needle and run it between the yarn wraps and the cardboard. Tie the ends in a knot as tightly as you can. If your knot is too loose, the pompom won't hold together, but be careful; if you pull your tying strand too hard the yarn could break.

5. Cut through all the wraps, on the opposite side of the cardboard from where you tied your knot. Holding it by the tied tails, fluff your pompom into a ball and give it a haircut, if needed, to make a nice round shape.

Pompom Maker
(page 136)

1 Open out both sides of the tool.

2 Beginning at one end of one side, wrap yarn around as many wraps as you wish (usually three or four passes back and forth).

3 Carry the yarn over to the other side of the tool and wrap (same number of wraps).

4 Close the sides of the tool.

5 Cut the pompom in the center groove on both sides of the tool. Cut the working yarn.

6 Cut a 10" (25 cm) length of yarn and tie it around the center groove.

7 Remove the tool, fluff the pompom, and trim.

Sewing

Often, the last step in a knitting project is to do some simple hand sewing, using a sewing needle and thread that matches your project.

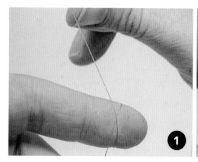
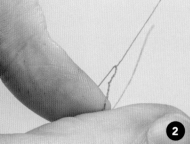
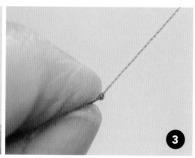

Tie a Knot

After threading the needle, double the thread over so the ends are even and tie a knot, like this:

1 Wrap the thread around the end of your index finger once.

2 Pinch the wrapped thread between your thumb and index finger, and roll it off the end of your index finger, forming a knot.

3 Keeping the knot pinched between your thumb and index finger, slide it down the thread to tighten.

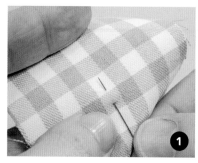

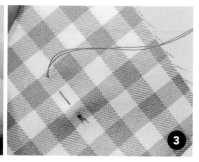

Running Stitch

1 Stab the needle straight down through all layers, then bring it up again about 1/8" (3 mm) away.

2 Repeat steps 1 for several stitches.

3 Pull the thread all the way through to the front side of the work.

4 Repeat steps 1 to 3 until you have all the stitches you need. Secure the thread by running the needle under the last stitch, and looping it around the needle before pulling the thread all the way through. Cut the thread.

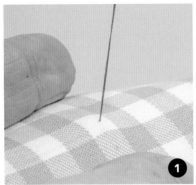  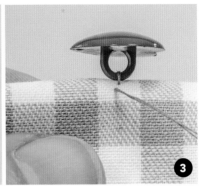

Buttons

1 At the desired button location, make a small stitch by sticking the needle point into and then out of the fabric, from the right side. Pull the thread all the way through.

2 Thread the needle through the shank of the button.

3 Repeat steps 1 and 2 three or four times, until the button feels secure.

4 Secure the thread as for running stitch, above.

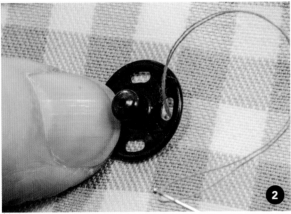 

Snaps

1 At the desired snap location, make a small stitch by sticking the needle point into and then out of the fabric, from the right side. Pull the thread all the way through.

2 Thread the needle through one piece of the snap and pull through.

3 Make three or four stitches through each of the holes in the snap.

4 Secure the thread as for running stitch, above.

5 Repeat steps 1 through 4 for the second half of the snap.

The Language of Knitting

Understanding the mechanics of how to make stitches is only the first part of becoming a knitter. Can you knit without a pattern? Of course. You can strum a guitar without knowing how to read music, and you can prepare food without using a cookbook, too. At some point, though, you will begin to run into limitations. Most knitters quickly reach a level of experience where they want to make more interesting and complicated projects, and for those, you need to understand the language of knitting.

Just as music has notes to read or cooking has recipes to follow, knitting patterns use their own special language to tell you how to make a project. While the layout and order of knitting patterns can vary, they all should contain the same basic elements. Each of the pattern parts provides you with information you need to successfully recreate the project. Even if you decide to change one or more things in your own version (knitters usually do!), it helps to know exactly how the original was made.

Parts of a Pattern

Title

Every knitting pattern has a name. Some names simply describe the project, while others strive to evoke the mood, history, or shape of the design. Pattern titles help you refer to your specific project when you are looking for further information, whether from other knitters, in books, or online.

Introduction

The introduction can tell you what inspired the designer, how the project is constructed, what is special about the pattern, and much more. Reading the introduction will help you understand more about your project.

Yarn

Every knitting pattern describes specifically, the exact yarn(s) used in the original. The manufacturer, skein yardage, weight, and colors will all be noted. If different amounts of yarn are needed for different sizes, that information will be listed under the yarn heading. This information is crucial, whether you plan to use the same yarn as the designer or make your own substitution. See more about yarn, fiber, and substitutions on page 30.

Needles

Your pattern will specify the precise size(s) of needles the designer used to create the original project. While you may ultimately decide that a different size works better for you, using the size stated in your pattern is a good place to start when making your test swatches. Learn more about swatching on page 36.

Gauge

Gauge is the description of exactly how many stitches and how many rows are in a 4" (10 cm) square of the original knitted piece. The only way to predict the finished size of your project is to exactly reproduce the designer's stated gauge. Keep in mind that the designer's gauge may or may not be different from the manufacturer's suggested gauge found on your yarn label, though they usually are close. More information about gauge can be found on page 32.

Notions

Notions are any items you'll need to complete your project, apart from yarn and needles. Stitch markers, tapestry needles, buttons, and stitch holders are all examples of typical notions called for in patterns. It's worthwhile to check this heading at the beginning of your project to make sure you have any unusual items on hand before you begin. Look at page 132 for further information on notions and tools that are useful for knitters.

Sizes and Finished Measurements

Patterns for items that can be made in different sizes (such as garments) list the size choices available. Each size should also have its corresponding finished measurements listed. It's not uncommon for knitting pattern sizes to be different from commercially made garment sizes, so look carefully at the actual finished measurements. For example, if you usually wear size medium, check to see if the pattern's measurements for that size are the same as your body (or a similar item of clothing that fits you).

Pattern Notes/Special Stitches

Not all patterns contain pattern notes, but sometimes designers need to tell you something specific about a stitch pattern, construction, or technique called for. When they do, you'll find it listed in this area, right before the beginning of the instructions.

(continued)

Instructions

The actual knitting instructions are usually somewhere near the middle of the pattern, after all the above elements are listed. In order to save space, the words used in instructions are mostly abbreviations, which can look strange and confusing at first. The full meaning of every abbreviation used in your pattern should be listed on the last pattern page, or if your pattern is in a book, in a separate chapter.

Take your time when you read instructions, stopping to look up each abbreviation. Some abbreviations are used so often, you'll learn to recognize them right away, such as "k" for knit, and "st" for stitch. Other abbreviations are used less often, and even experienced knitters have to stop and look them up to make sure they understand. For every knitter, a good rule of thumb is: When in doubt, check it out. It only takes a minute to make sure, and before long you'll know most abbreviations by heart.

Instructions are usually broken down into paragraphs with headings that indicate the order of construction, such as "Lower Edge," "Body," and "Sleeves." Under each heading, the steps for each phase are described, in sentences.

The sentences in knitting instructions are intended to be followed one at a time. Each phrase describes a step in the knitting process, ending with a period. It's good to work slowly, remembering that you only have to make sure you understand one sentence at a time.

EXAMPLE

With smaller needles and CC, CO 60 sts. Work in k1, p1 rib until piece measures 1" (2.5 cm) from beg. With larger needles and MC, work in St st until piece measures 6" (15 cm) from beg.

TRANSLATION

1 With the smallest needle size listed at the beginning of the pattern and the contrast color (described under the yarn heading), cast on 60 stitches.

2 Alternate knit and purl stitches to create a ribbed edge (check the photo if you're not sure what the edge should look like). Work as many rows of ribbing as it takes to make your piece of knitting 1" (or 2.5 cm) from the bottom edge to the top of the needle, when lying flat.

3 Change to the larger size needle listed at the beginning and the main color of yarn, then knit in stockinette stitch (knit on right side rows, purl on wrong side rows), until your piece has enough rows to measure 6" (15 cm) long from the beginning (more details about measuring are on page 38).

Charts

In order to save space, some knitting patterns have charts that represent how each stitch in every row should be worked. To knit from a chart, you read each line row by row, from the bottom up, with each square on the chart referring to an individual stitch. Learn more about following charts on page 65.

Photos

In addition to showing you what the finished project looks like, the photos in knitting patterns are carefully selected to help the knitter see important elements. The shape of a sock toe, the location of a buttonhole, or the way a shawl is tied can all be helpful clues to you as you work. Remember to look more closely at the pattern photos if you're feeling confused about anything.

Schematics

Another visual aid provided by your designer, schematics are simple line drawings that clearly show you both the shape and the measurements of various elements. Schematics make it easier to see the exact shaping and construction of a project than photos do. See page 66 for more on reading schematics.

Abbreviations

If your pattern is part of a book or collection of designs, all abbreviations used in the book should be listed alphabetically, in their own chapter. If your pattern was published individually, a list of all the abbreviations used should appear at the end of the pattern. Abbreviations for the patterns in this book begin on page 141.

Reading Charts

Pictures can often give us more concise information in a smaller space than words do. Some charts show a pattern of stitches that is meant to be repeated a given number of times. Others, such as this one for the inside of the Kitty Ears, show how to work each individual stitch in the whole piece.

Each row of blocks in the chart represents a row of stitches. Each individual block corresponds to a single stitch. The numbers to the right of the chart tell us which row is which, and the symbols in each block represent a knitting action.

Just like maps, charts include keys for identifying their symbols. The key for our Kitty Ears chart explains what each block in the chart is telling us to do.

Charts are always worked from the bottom to the top. Charts for flat knitting (like this one) are worked from left to right on right side rows, and right to left on wrong side rows. So when we follow this chart, we can see:

Row 1: Knit 19 stitches.

Row 2: Purl 19 stitches.

Row 3: Knit 1 stitch, decrease 1 stitch using SSK (slip, slip, knit), knit 13 stitches, decrease 1 stitch using k2tog (knit 2 stitches together).

Row 4: Purl 17 stitches.

And so on, all the way to the end of the piece. Each time we come to a block with a symbol in it, we perform the knitting action it calls for.

Once you understand how to read them, charts provide a simple and elegant way to see the steps required for your knitting. You can even knit from charts written in other languages. Japanese knitting patterns contain no written instructions, only charts. Once decoded, the symbols tell knitters stitch by stitch how to knit the pattern, no matter what language they speak.

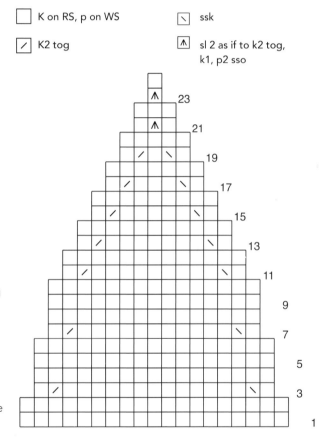

K on RS, p on WS

K2 tog

ssk

sl 2 as if to k2 tog, k1, p2 sso

Reading Schematics

While the photographs provided with patterns tell you how the finished project will look, they can't provide all the specific information you need to understand its shaping and construction. For that you need a special illustration, called a "schematic." Schematics are greatly simplified line drawings designed to clarify the exact shape and measurements of the piece you are knitting. Comparing the schematic drawing to the written instructions can help clarify the way your project is constructed as you work.

Schematics don't show details like collars or edgings, only the basic shape of each main piece. In the example here, you can tell that the dog sweater is knitted in one piece, and that its upper edge curves around the dog's neck in a U-shape. The measurements shown correspond to the areas of garter stitch and stockinette stitch called for in the written instructions.

All the measurements for different sizes are listed in the schematic, which can be helpful when you are deciding which size to knit. While the size and measurement information at the beginning of the pattern tells you in words, the schematic shows you in a picture. In our dog sweater example, if you wanted to know how wide the lower edge would be for small, medium, and large sizes, you would simply check the bottom of the schematic where those measurements are listed.

After the knitting is complete, the schematic will also help you block your finished piece to its proper measurements. Once knitting has been wetted with steam or by washing, it can stretch out of shape. Referring to the schematic will help you return it to its proper dimensions for drying.

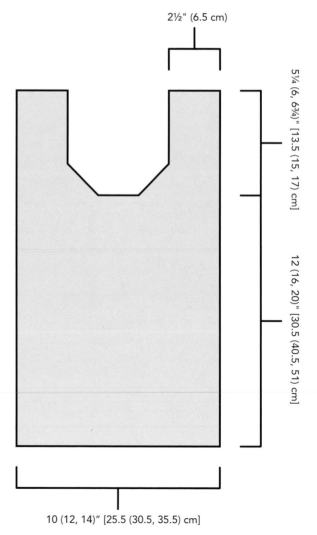

2½" (6.5 cm)

5¼ (6, 6¾)" [13.5 (15, 17) cm]

12 (16, 20)" [30.5 (40.5, 51) cm]

10 (12, 14)" [25.5 (30.5, 35.5) cm]

Before You Knit

Help get your knitting off to a great start by taking these few simple steps before you begin of your new project.

READ THE PATTERN ALL THE WAY THROUGH.

Even if you don't understand every individual step at first, reading all the instructions before you start knitting will give you a general idea of how the project is made, and the order of its construction.

1 MAKE A COPY.

If your pattern is contained in a book, making a photocopy will keep your book from getting beat up and written in, and allow you to transport your pattern along with your project more easily. When you photocopy your pattern, you can even enlarge it, for easier reading. Some knitters like to purchase digital copies of knitting patterns, and use a digital tablet to knit from, so they never have to make paper copies.

2 HIGHLIGHT YOUR SIZE.

Check each step in your instructions for different sizing. It looks like this:

CO 30 (36, 42, 48) sts.

This instruction is showing you that different sizes call for different numbers of stitches to be cast on. The smallest size is always shown first, then larger sizes in increasing order, inside the parentheses. Every time you see parentheses ( ), carefully select the size you'll be knitting and circle it, mark it with a highlighter pen, or otherwise make it clear for yourself which is the number pertaining to your size.

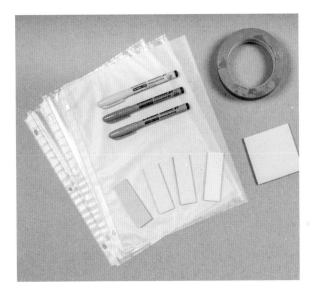

3 MARK YOUR PLACE.

Use sticky notes, a magnetic holder, or painter's masking tape (with a plastic document sleeve) to keep track of where you are in the pattern instructions. It's easy to get confused when you accidentally start reading the wrong area or page of your pattern or come back to your knitting after taking a break.

4 Taking a few minutes to prepare your pattern like this will set you up for success and make knitting more fun.

Projects

And now for the fun stuff! Why not begin by making your own knitting needles? The fourteen knitting projects that follow are arranged in order of difficulty, and the skills you'll need are listed, so be sure to go back and review before you cast on. If you begin by knitting friendship bracelets and knit your way through to making a sweater, you will tackle and conquer a wide range of knitting challenges, developing your skills along the way.

Handmade Knitting Needles

Making your own knitting needles is a great way to get a pair that's perfect for you. Store-bought needles are almost always both the same color, but when you make your own, you can color each one differently. Being able to tell easily which needle is which can be a big help when you're first learning to knit.

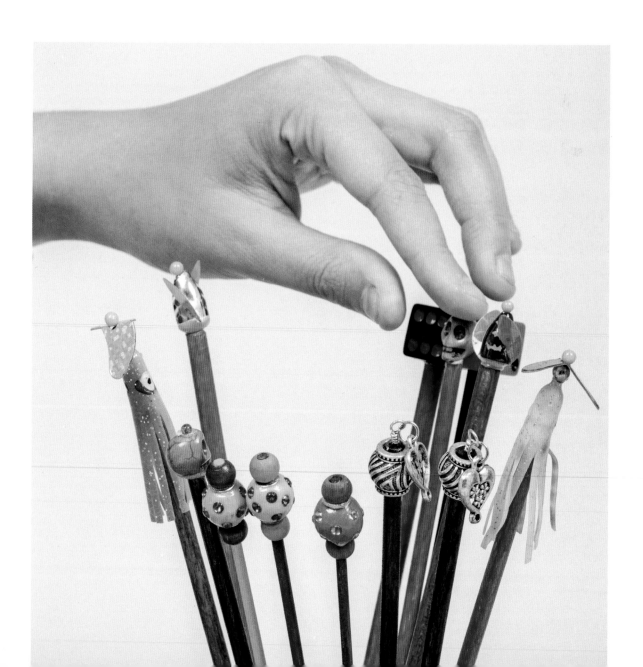

You will need

Materials

- ⅛" dowel(s) for size US 3 (3.25 mm) needles

- ³/₁₆" dowel(s) for size US 8 (5 mm) needles

- ¼" dowel(s) for size US 10 (6 mm) needles

- Sandpaper sheets in 320 and 400 grits

- Permanent markers (at least two colors)

- Clear spray lacquer

- Clear craft glue (such as Beacon 3-in-1)

- Beads, toys, game pieces, erasers, fishing lures, etc., for finials

- Round-head sewing pins

Tools

- Multisize rotary pencil sharpener

- Ruler or tape measure

- Pencil

- Penknife or craft knife

- Paper towel or rag

- Small vase or cup to stand needles in as they dry

- Power drill

- Pliers or vise to hold small pieces for drilling

- Wire cutters

You can make straight needles in pairs for flat knitting, or double-pointed needles in sets of five for circular (tubular) knitting. Straight needles have stoppers, or finials, on their ends to keep the knitting from sliding off. Double-pointed needles (dpn) don't have any stoppers, so you can knit from either of their ends.

Most of the projects in this book can be worked on needles of the following sizes: US 3 (3.25 mm), US 8 (5 mm), and US 10 (6 mm). You can buy hardwood dowels at home centers, craft stores, and online. They usually come in 36" (91.5 cm) or 48" (122 cm) lengths. Have fun hunting in craft stores, sporting goods stores, or even your own toy collection for items to use as finials. Anything that can be drilled, glued, or stuck through with a pin can become a needle end! Remember kids will need the help of an adult when using paint, glue, and sharp tools.

Straight Needles

Begin by covering your work surface to protect it from markers and lacquer. Working outside is best, if possible. Wear old clothes, too, in case of marker accidents. Assemble all your tools and materials.

Form Points and Cut

Sharpen the end of a dowel in the pencil sharpener before cutting the needle to length, in case you need to redo the point. One person should support the end of the long dowel while the other sharpens the point. Be careful to hold the dowel straight (not at an angle) so the needle's point will be centered. When you are happy with the needle point, place the dowel flat on your work surface. Measure 10" (25.5 cm) from the point of the needle and mark a cutting line with your pencil. Using the penknife or craft knife, score a line around the dowel. Snap the dowel off at the score. Make a second needle to match.

tip Don't worry too much if your needles aren't perfectly smooth. It's actually knitting with them that makes needles silky smooth, over time.

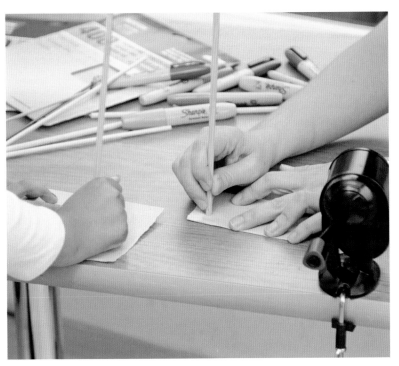

Finish Points and Sand

If needed, use the penknife to finish and smooth the points (more likely to be needed on the smallest needle size). Using the 320-grit sandpaper, sand the cut ends of each needle smooth. Gently sand the sides of the point, holding the needle like a pencil and rotating it after every few strokes. The point of the needle should be very sharp now—too sharp to knit with, actually. Hold the needle straight up, with its point on the sandpaper. Gently rub in tiny circles to blunt the tip. Now carefully sand the needle shaft, rolling it back and forth inside the sandpaper to avoid forming ridges. Repeat all the steps on both needles, this time using the 400-grit sandpaper.

Color Your Needles

Using a rag or paper towel, carefully dust the needles. Choose two markers to color the needles. Starting at the point, carefully color your needle with a marker, all the way around. Work down the length of the needle about halfway, making sure not to miss any spots. Place the needle in a cup to dry while you color the second needle the same way, with a different marker. Return to the first needle and color the other half of it. Set it aside to dry and repeat with the second needle and marker.

Finish the Surface

Once the ink is dry on both needles, it's time to seal them with spray lacquer. Hold both needles side by side in one hand with your fingers in between to keep them from touching. Spray the exposed ends lightly with lacquer. Turn your hand over and lightly spray the other sides of the needles. Carefully place them in a cup (with the unsprayed ends down, and not touching each other) to dry. Once the sprayed ends are dry (check the drying time on the can), reverse the needles in your hands and spray the other ends. Repeat this process two more times, for a total of three very light coats on each end of both needles.

Add Finials

If your finials need drilling to fit on the ends of your needles, have an adult do the job. A vise is the best tool to hold small pieces for drilling. If you don't have a vise, one adult can hold the piece to be drilled firmly with pliers, while another adult uses the power drill to make the hole. Once the finial pieces have holes to fit your needles, add a dab of craft glue to the end of each needle and spread it all the way around the shaft. Add each finial and set aside to dry.

Some beads and finial pieces (such as fishing lures) are best attached to the needles with shortened sewing pins. Place the pin through the piece and hold it up next to the end of the knitting needle to estimate how much to shorten the pin. The pin only needs to go about ½" (1.3 cm) into the wood. Use wire cutters to cut the pin off at an angle, at the desired length. Add one drop of glue to the end of the needle, and another to the pin. Carefully drive the pin through the finial piece and into the center of the needle end. Allow the needles to dry overnight before using them.

Double-Pointed Needles (DPN)

Make dpn exactly the same way as for straight needles, but without adding finials. After sharpening the first end, cut the needle to a length of 8" (20.5 cm) and sharpen the opposite end. Make four more needles, for a set of five. Sand and finish your dpn as for straights, choosing a different color for each one, if desired.

tips The needle lengths given are the standard lengths found in purchased needles. Feel free to make your needles the length you like best, or need for your project.

Handmade knitting needles make great gifts for your knitting friends. Top them with finials that have special meaning for each person.

Friendship Bracelets

Knitted projects rely on the three basic skills of casting on, knitting, and binding off. Friendship bracelets allow you to practice all three, and they are fun and quick to make. Knit them in solid colors or stripes, narrow or wide. Ask other knitters for odds and ends of medium-weight yarn, or get together with friends to share skeins. You can adjust the size of each bracelet by changing the location of the snaps.

You will need

Yarn

 Medium

SHOWN: Classic Wool Worsted by Patons, 100% wool, 3.5 oz (100 g)/210 yd (192 m): Bright Red #00230 (CA), Royal Blue #77132 (CB), and Magenta #77402 (CC), about 10 yd (10 m) each

Needles

- Size 8 (5 mm) straight or size to obtain gauge

Notions

- Tapestry needle

- Three size 3 (½" [1.3 cm]) snaps

- Hand sewing needle and thread

Gauge

19 sts and 32 rows = 4" (10 cm) in garter st
Take time to check gauge.

Sizes

Wide Bracelet

Finished measurements: 8½" (21.5 cm) long, 1½" (3.8 cm) high

Narrow Bracelet

Finished measurements: 8½" (21.5 cm) long, ½" (1.3 cm) high

Construction

Bracelets are worked back and forth in rows.

Stitch Guide

GARTER STITCH: Knit every st, every row.

Wide Bracelet

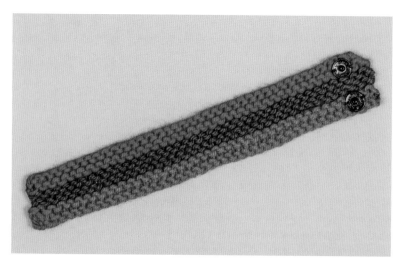

With CA and using the long-tail CO method, CO 40 sts. Knit 4 rows. Break yarn and join CB using a weaver's knot. Knit 4 rows. Break yarn and join CC. Knit 3 rows. BO.

Finishing

Weave in ends. Block to measurements. Sew 2 snap halves to each end of bracelet as shown with hand sewing needle and thread.

Narrow Bracelet

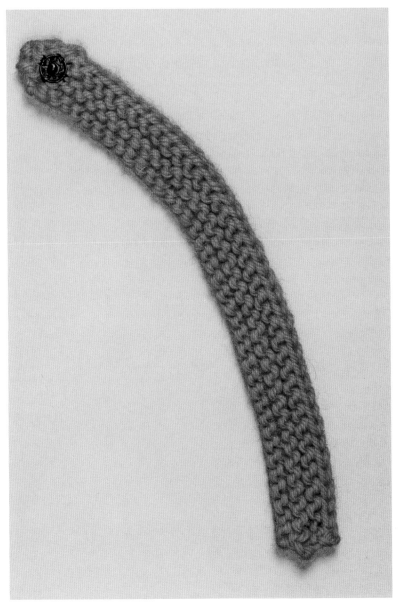

tip Embellish your finished bracelets by sewing on buttons, beads, or silk flowers after knitting.

Cast On, page 10
Knit, page 16
Weaver's Knot, page 44
Bind Off, page 20
Weave Ends, page 49
Blocking, page 52
Snaps, page 61

Work as for wide bracelet in the color of your choice, binding off at the end of the first stripe. Use 1 snap for narrow bracelet.

Felted Coasters

Coasters are something everybody can use, and these are especially nice because they are both absorbent and washable. Coasters don't require much yarn, and you can make sets in matching, or any combination of, colors. This project is useful for practicing garter stitch. One of the great things about felted knitting is that small mistakes and irregularities in your stitches will disappear into the finished felt. Magic!

You will need

Yarn

 Medium

SHOWN: Cascade 220 by Cascade Yarns, 100% Peruvian Highland wool, 3.5 oz (100 g)/220 yd (201 m): Blue Hawaii #9421, Chartreuse #7814, Anis #8908, and Como Blue #9420, about 70 yd (64 m) each

Needles

- Size 10 (6 mm) straight or size to obtain gauge

Notions

- Tapestry needle

Gauge

16 sts and 32 rows = 4" (10 cm) in garter st, before felting. Take time to check gauge.

Sizes

Finished measurements: About 5½" (14 cm) high, 4½" (11.5 cm) wide

Construction

Coasters are worked from the bottom up, back and forth in rows.

Stitch Guide

GARTER STITCH: Knit every st, every row.

Coaster
(make 1 in each color)

CO 30 sts. Work 60 rows in garter st. BO.

Finishing

Weave in ends. Felt coasters. Shape as desired and lay coasters flat to dry.

Cast On, page 10
Knit, page 16
Bind Off, page 20
Weave Ends, page 49
Felting, page 54

Favorite Washcloth

Hand knitted washcloths are wonderful to use, because they get softer and softer with age. They are also quick and fun to knit, which makes them excellent for gift giving. Washcloths are so popular to make that many yarn companies keep a line of cotton washcloth yarns in their collections at all times. This project will help you practice yo (yarn over) increases, k2tog (knit two together) decreases, and garter stitch knitting. Be warned, though—once you start making washcloths, you (and the people you give them to) might get hooked on them!

You will need

Yarn

 Medium

SHOWN: Kitchen Cotton by Lion Brand, 100% cotton, 2 oz (57 g)/99 yd (91 m): Kiwi #831-170, 1 skein

Needles

- Size 8 (5 mm) straight or size to obtain gauge

Notions

- Tapestry needle

Gauge

18 sts and 36 rows = 4" (10 cm) in garter st

Take time to check gauge.

Sizes

Finished measurements: 9½" (24 cm) tall, 9½" (24 cm) wide

Construction

Washcloth is worked diagonally from point to point, back and forth in rows.

Stitch Guide

GARTER STITCH: Knit every st, every row.

Washcloth

CO 4 sts. Knit 2 rows.

Increases

Inc row: *K2, yo, knit to end of row—1 st inc'd.
Rep inc row every row 55 more times—60 sts.

Decreases

Dec row: *K1, k2tog, yo, k2tog, knit to end of row—
1 st dec'd.
Rep dec row every row 53 more times—6 sts.

Next row: K1, [k2tog] 2 times, k1—4 sts.
Knit 2 rows. BO.

Finishing

Weave in ends. Block to measurements.

Cast On, page 10
Knit, page 16
Increases, page 25
Decreases, page 26
Bind Off, page 20
Weave Ends, page 49
Blocking, page 52

tip To make a yarn over (yo), bring the working yarn forward between the needles, then lay it from front to back over the top of the right needle. That's all there is to it!

Slippers

Cozy toes are only a few stitches away! Slippers are fun and fast to knit, especially in bulky weight yarn, like this. Practice garter stitch; k1, p1 rib; and k2tog in this project.

You will need

Yarn

 5 Bulky

SHOWN: Wool of the Andes Bulky by Knit Picks, 100% Peruvian Highland wool, 3.5 oz (100 g)/137 yd (125 m): Wine #23964, 1 skein

Needles

- Size 10 (6 mm) straight or size to obtain gauge

Notions

- Tapestry needle
- 1 yd (1 m) of ¾" (19 mm) velvet ribbon (shown: May Arts PV25, burgundy)
- Two ⅞" x ⅝" (2.2 x 1.6 cm) buttons
- Hand sewing needle and thread

Gauge

16 sts and 32 rows = 4" (10 cm) in garter st

Take time to check gauge.

Sizes

Finished size: about 7" (18 cm) foot circumference

Construction

Slippers are worked from heel to toe, back and forth in rows.

Stitch Guide

GARTER STITCH: Knit every st, every row.

K1, P1 RIB: RS rows: *K1, p1; rep from * to last st, k1.

WS rows: *P1, k1; rep from * to last st, p1.

Slippers

To make your slippers the right size, have a friend help you measure your foot like this:

1 Place a piece of paper on a hard floor (not carpeted), then step onto it.

2 Have your helper place a ruler on its edge against the back of your heel, then draw a line against it.

3 Don't move, while your helper places the ruler against your toes the same way, to draw another line. The distance between the two lines is your foot measurement.

4 CO 29 sts, leaving a 12" (30.5 cm) tail. Work in garter st until piece measures 3" (7.5 cm) less than foot measurement. Work in k1, p1 rib until piece measures ½" (1.3 cm) less than foot measurement, ending with a WS row.

Next row (RS): K1, [k2tog] 14 times—15 sts.

Break yarn, leaving a 12" (30.5 cm) tail. Thread yarn tail through tapestry needle, and run needle through rem live sts, pulling snugly to gather. Fasten yarn securely on WS. Without breaking yarn, sew toe seam closed using mattress st, fastening securely at beg of garter st. Break yarn. Fold slipper in half lengthwise, bringing 2 halves of CO edge tog at heel. Using CO tail, sew CO edges tog with mattress st at heel.

Finishing

Weave in ends. Cut 2 lengths of ribbon, each about 15" (38 cm) long. Cross the ends to form a bow shape (see illustration). Sew through all layers at center as shown and pull thread tightly to gather. Sew bow to slipper through center. Sew button over center of bow. Trim ends of ribbon diagonally.

Cast On, page 10
Knit, page 16
Purl, page 18
Decreases, page 26
Weave Ends, page 49
Mattress Stitch, page 46

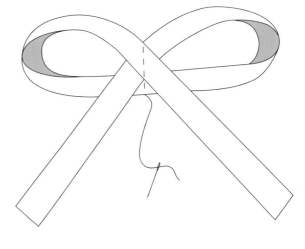

tip These slippers are great for guys as well; just omit the ribbons.

Cowl

Cowls are terrific for practicing knitting in the round. They take much less time to make than scarves, but provide the same cuddly function! Try this one to master k2, p2 rib and stockinette in the round.

You will need

Yarn

 Medium

SHOWN: Longwood by Cascade Yarns, 100% superwash extrafine merino wool, 3.5 oz (100 g)/191 yd (175 m): Plum #28 (MC) and Green Olive #15 (CC), 1 skein each

Needles

- Size 7 (4.5 mm) 16" (40 cm) circular

- Size 8 (5 mm) 16" (40 cm) circular or size to obtain gauge

Notions

- Stitch marker

- Tapestry needle

Gauge

20 sts and 27 rnds = 4" (10 cm) in St st on larger needle

Take time to check gauge.

Sizes

Finished measurements: 18½" (47 cm) circumference, 10" (25.5 cm) high

Construction

Cowl is worked circularly, in rounds, from bottom to top.

Stitch Guide

K2, P2 RIB: *K2, p2; rep from * to end of rnd.

STOCKINETTE STITCH (ST ST): Knit every st, every rnd.

Cowl

With smaller needle, CC, and using the cable CO method, CO 92 sts. Pm and join for working in rnds, being careful not to twist. Work in k2, p2 rib until piece measures 1" (2.5 cm) from CO. Break yarn and join MC. With larger needle, work in St st until piece measures 9" (23 cm) from CO. Break yarn and join CC. Knit 1 rnd. Work in k2, p2 rib until piece measures 10" (25.5 cm) from CO. BO loosely in patt.

Finishing

Weave in ends. Steam lightly to block.

Cast On, page 10
Join a Round, page 29
Knit, page 16
Purl, page 18
Bind Off, page 20
Weave Ends, page 49
Blocking, page 52

tip "Binding off in pattern" means that you work each stitch in the bind off as it was worked in the prior round: bind off knit stitches knitwise, and bind off purl stitches purlwise.

Pompom Hat

Here's a great project to practice knitting in the round. The simple shape easily fits various sizes, and its loose-fitting style can be worn lots of different ways. The rolled edge; k1, p1 rib; and three-needle bind off are all techniques you'll use again and again. And of course, don't forget the pompoms!

You will need

Yarn

 Medium

SHOWN: Cascade 220 by Cascade Yarns, 100% Peruvian Highland wool, 3.5 oz (100 g)/220 yd (201 m): Blue Hawaii #9421, 1 skein (MC); Chartreuse #7814, 1 skein (CA); Anis #8908 (CB) and Como Blue #9420 (CC), about 8 yd (7 m) each

Needles

- Size 8 (5 mm) 16" (40 cm) circular or size to obtain gauge

Notions

- Spare circular needle in same size or smaller than main needle

- Stitch marker

- Tapestry needle

- Small (1⅝" [4 cm]) Clover pompom maker or scrap cardboard

Gauge

20 sts and 28 rnds = 4" (10 cm) in St st

Take time to check gauge.

Sizes

Finished measurements: 20" (51 cm) circumference, 8½" (21.5 cm) high

Construction

Hat is worked from the bottom up, in rounds.

Stitch Guide

STOCKINETTE STITCH (ST ST): Knit every st, every rnd.

K1, P1 RIB: *K1, p1; rep from * to end of rnd.

Hat

Lower Edge

With CA, CO 100 sts. Pm and join for working in rnds, being careful not to twist. Knit 6 rnds. Work 6 rnds in k1, p1 rib. Break yarn.

Body

Join MC and work in St st until piece measures 7½" (19 cm) from color change. Do not BO.

Finishing

Top Seam

Turn hat inside out and place 50 sts onto spare needle. Work three-needle BO.

Weave in ends. Block hat, allowing lower edge to roll to RS. Make 2 pompoms each in CA, CB, and CC. Sew 3 pompoms to each corner of hat.

Cast On, page 10
Join a Round, page 29
Knit, page 16
Purl, page 18
Three-Needle Bind Off, page 47
Weave Ends, page 49
Blocking, page 52
Pompoms, page 56

Felted Bag

Knitted bags can be made in any shape and size you like. Felting the finished bag will make it strong and sturdy enough to safely transport your treasures. Before felting, your bag might seem gigantic, but felting will magically transform it to the perfect size. Experiment with different color combinations, embellishments, and straps for totally different looks. Don't be surprised when all your friends ask for one, too.

You will need

Yarn

 Bulky

SHOWN: Wool of the Andes Bulky by Knit Picks, 100% Peruvian Highland wool, 3.5 oz (100 g)/137 yd (125 m): Crush #25952 (CA), Avocado #25958 (CB), and Masala #24681 (CC), 1 skein each

Needles

- Size 15 (10 mm) 24" (60 cm) circular or size to obtain gauge

Notions

- Stitch marker

- Spare circular needle in same size or smaller than main needle

- Tapestry needle

- 32" (81.5 cm) leather purse straps (shown: Cindy's Button Company #1006 Mum)

- Hand sewing needle and thread

Gauge

9 sts and 13 rnds = 4" (10 cm) in St st, before felting

Take time to check gauge.

Sizes

Finished measurements (before felting): 18" (45.5 cm) high, 22¼" (56.5 cm) wide

Finished measurements (after felting): 9½" (24 cm) high, 14" (35.5 cm) wide

Construction

Bag is worked circularly, in rounds, from top to bottom.

Stitch Guide

K1, P1 RIB: *K1, p1; rep from * to end of rnd.

STOCKINETTE STITCH (ST ST): Knit every st, every rnd.

Bag

With CA, CO 100 sts. Pm and join for working in rnds, being careful not to twist. Work 6 rnds in k1, p1 rib. Work in St st until piece measures 6" (15 cm) from CO. Break CA and join CB. Work in St st until piece measures 12" (30.5 cm) from CO. Break CB and join CC. Work in St st until piece measures 18" (45.5 cm) from CO. Do not BO.

Finishing

Bottom Seam

Turn bag inside out. With WS facing, place 50 sts on spare circular needle. With CC, work three-needle BO to close seam. Weave in ends.

Felt bag. Sew straps securely to each side of bag as shown.

Cast On, page 10
Join a Round, page 29
Knit, page 16
Purl, page 18
Three-Needle Bind Off, page 47
Weave Ends, page 49
Felting, page 54

tip Ribbon, cords, and even recycled belts can all make interesting purse straps.

Cozy Scarf

At some point or another, every knitter wants to make a scarf. And why not? They're simple, cuddly, and as much fun to wear as they are to knit. Here's a great one to start with. Worked in soft, chunky wool, its big gauge makes it quick to knit. Practice stockinette stitch and slipping stitches at the beginning of each row to keep the edges tidy. Finish the ends with jaunty pompoms for a touch of whimsy!

You will need

 5 Bulky

 4 Medium

SHOWN: Chunky by Malabrigo, 100% merino wool, 3.5 oz (100 g)/104 yd (95 m): Tiger Lily #152 (MC), 2 skeins

- Cascade 220 by Cascade Yarns, 100% Peruvian Highland wool, 3.5 oz (100 g)/220 yd (201 m): Chartreuse #7814 (CA), Blue Hawaii #9421 (CB), Anis #8908 (CC), and Como Blue #9420 (CD), about 8 yd (7 m) each

Needles

- Size 10 (6 mm) straight or size to obtain gauge

Notions

- Tapestry needle
- Small (1⅝" [4 cm]) Clover pompom maker or scrap cardboard

Gauge

14 sts and 20 rows = 4" (10 cm) in St st with MC

Take time to check gauge.

Sizes

Finished measurements: 46" (117 cm) long, 8½" (21.5 cm) wide

Construction

Scarf is worked back and forth in rows.

Stitch Guide

STOCKINETTE STITCH (ST ST): RS rows: Knit. WS rows: Purl.

Scarf

With MC, CO 30 sts. Slipping first st of every row (with yarn in back on RS rows and with yarn in front on WS rows), work in St st until piece measures 46" (117 cm) from CO, or to desired length. BO.

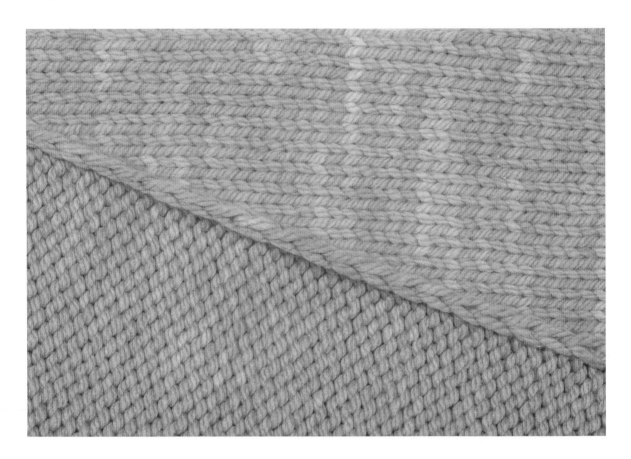

Finishing

Weave in ends. Block scarf. Make 2 pompoms each in CA, CB, CC, and CD. Sew 4 pompoms to each end of scarf, as shown.

Cast On, page 10
Slip a Stitch, page 45
Knit, page 16
Purl, page 18
Bind Off, page 20
Weave Ends, page 49
Blocking, page 52
Pompoms, page 56

Kitty Ears

Feel a little feline? Pop on your Kitty Ears. These ears are a fun way to practice decreases: left-leaning (ssk), right-leaning (k2tog), and centered double (sl2-k1-p2sso) are all used here. Follow the charts line by line to make four triangles. Then felt them in your washing machine and sew together. Cover a headband with knitted cord and attach the ears. You'll look great on the catwalk.

You will need

Yarn

 Medium

SHOWN: Cascade 220 by Cascade Yarns, 100% Peruvian Highland wool, 3.5 oz (100 g)/220 yd (201 m): Silver Grey #8401 (MC), 1 skein; Soft Pink #4192 (CC), 1 skein

Needles

- Size 10 (6 mm) straight or size to obtain gauge

- Size 6 (4 mm) set of dpn

Notions

- Tapestry needle

- ³⁄₈" (10 mm) wide plastic headband

- Hand sewing needle and thread

Gauge

14 sts and 20 rows = 4" (10 cm) in St st on larger needles, before felting

Take time to check gauge.

Sizes

Finished measurements: Each ear = 3½" (9 cm) high, 3" (7.5 cm) wide

Construction

The outer and inner ears are knit separately from the bottom up, then felted and sewn together. Knitted cord covers the headband.

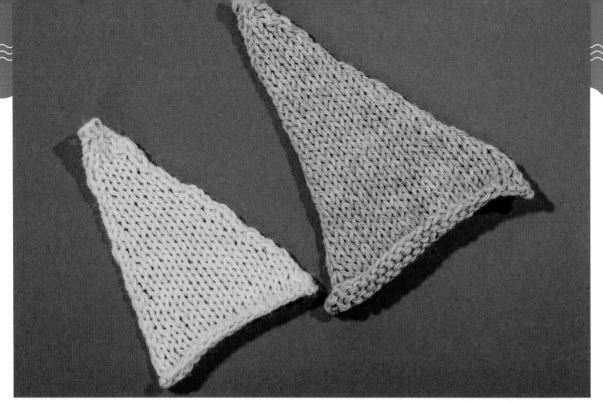

Outer Ears (make 2)

With larger needles and MC, CO 25 sts. Work Rows 1–30 of Outer Ear chart. Break yarn and thread tail through last st.

Inner Ears (make 2)

With larger needles and CC, CO 19 sts. Work Rows 1–24 of Inner Ear chart. Break yarn and thread tail through last st.

Headband Cover

With smaller dpn and MC, CO 4 sts. Work knitted cord to the same length as your headband (about 15" [38 cm]). Break yarn and thread tail through 4 live sts. Pull to inside of cord. Thread headband into cord. Close end of cord with tail from CO.

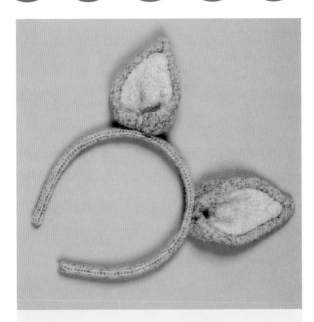

Key

☐	K on RS, p on WS	◹	ssk
◸	K2 tog	⋏	sl 2 as if to k2 tog, k1, p2 sso

[LS8695-102]

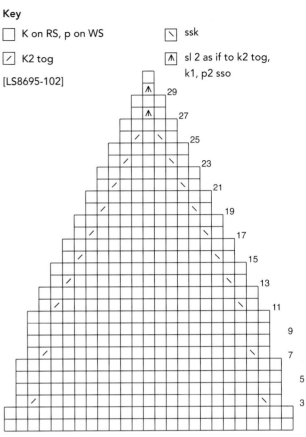

Outer Ear

tip To get a more catlike ear shape, steam each ear with an iron over the back of a soup ladle.

Finishing

Weave in ends. Felt all pieces as desired, including headband. After felting, shape ear pieces into triangles, and straighten headband cord, if necessary. Allow to air-dry.

Layer inner ears over outer ears, with WS tog. Sew both pairs tog invisibly by hand. Using four strands of sewing thread and hand sewing needle, make running stitches in lower edge of each ear and pull up tightly to gather. Knot gathering threads securely.

Try on headband and pin ears in place. Sew ears to headband, knotting thread securely.

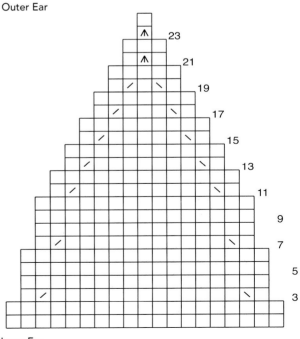

Inner Ear

Dog Sweater

Why not knit a sweater for your best friend? Here's a fun and easy one that will let you practice garter stitch, stockinette stitch, decreases, and making buttonholes. The buttons make it easy to put on and take off (provided you can get your dog to hold still). Measure your dog first to determine what size sweater to make.

You will need

Yarn

 Bulky

SHOWN: Wool of the Andes Bulky by Knit Picks, 100% Peruvian Highland wool, 3.5 oz (100 g)/137 yd (125 m): Red #25106, 2 (2, 3) skeins

Needles

- Size 10 (6 mm) straight or size to obtain gauge

Notions

- Stitch holder
- Tapestry needle
- Four 1" (2.5 cm) buttons
- Safety pins

Gauge

16 sts and 23 rows = 4" (10 cm) in St st

Take time to check gauge.

Sizes

Finished measurements: 17¼ (22, 26¾)" (44 [56, 68] cm) long, 10 (12, 14)" (25.5 [30.5, 35.5] cm) wide

NOTE: Size shown is 22" (56 cm) long.

Construction

Sweater is worked from lower edge to neck, back and forth in rows.

Stitch Guide

GARTER STITCH: Knit every st, every row.

STOCKINETTE STITCH (ST ST): RS rows: Knit. WS rows: Purl.

Sweater

Lower Edge

CO 40 (48, 56) sts. Work in garter st until piece measures 1" (2.5 cm) from CO, ending with a WS row.

Body

Next row (RS): Knit.
Next row (WS): K5, purl to last 5 sts, k5.

Rep last 2 rows until piece measures 11 (15, 19)" (28 [38, 48.5] cm) from CO, ending with a WS row. Work even in garter st until piece measures 12 (16, 20)" (30.5 [40.5, 51] cm) from CO, ending with a WS row.

Shape Neck

Next row (RS): K16 (19, 22) and place these sts on a holder for right strap, BO 8 (10, 12) sts, knit to end—16 (19, 22) sts for left strap.

Cont working on left strap sts only.

Left Strap

Next row (WS): Knit.
Next row (RS): K1, ssk, knit to end of row—1 st dec'd.

Rep last 2 rows 5 (8, 11) more times—10 sts. Work even in garter st until strap measures 6¼ (7, 7¾)" (16 [18, 19.5] cm) from beg of garter st. BO.

Right Strap

Return 16 (19, 22) sts to needle. With WS facing, rejoin yarn at neck edge and knit 1 row.

Next row (RS): Knit to last 3 sts, k2tog, k1—1 st dec'd.
Next row (WS): Knit.

Rep last 2 rows 5 (8, 11) more times—10 sts. Work even in garter st until strap measures 3¼ (4, 4¾)" (8.5 [10, 12] cm) from beg of garter st, ending with a WS row.

Buttonhole row (RS): K4, k2tog, yo, knit to end of row.

Work even until strap measures 5¼ (6, 6¾)" (13.5 [15, 17] cm) from beg of garter st, ending with a WS row. Rep buttonhole row. Work even until strap measures 6¼ (7, 7¾)" (16 [18, 19.5] cm) from beg of garter st. BO.

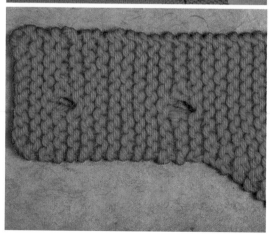

Chest Strap

CO 10 sts. Work even in garter st until strap measures ½" (1.3 cm), ending with a WS row.

Buttonhole row (RS): K4, k2tog, yo, knit to end of row.

Work even until strap measures 8 (9, 10)" (20.5 [23, 25.5] cm) from CO, ending with a WS row. Rep buttonhole row. Work even until strap measures 9 (10, 11)" (23 [25.5, 28] cm) from CO. BO.

Finishing

Weave in ends. Block to measurements. Place sweater on dog and mark locations for buttons on left neck strap and sides of body with pins. Sew buttons at marked locations.

Cast On, page 10
Knit, page 16
Purl, page 18
Decreases, page 26
Buttonhole, page 51
Bind Off, page 20
Weave Ends, page 49
Blocking, page 52
Buttons, page 61

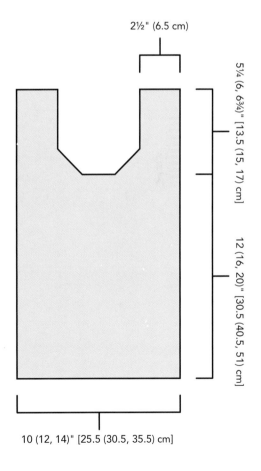

2½" (6.5 cm)

5¼ (6, 6¾)" [13.5 (15, 17) cm]

12 (16, 20)" [30.5 (40.5, 51) cm]

10 (12, 14)" [25.5 (30.5, 35.5) cm]

Bow Tie

Variegated yarns are specially dyed to create stripes when you knit. Try this hand-dyed version to make a dapper bow tie any fella will love. The neckband can be made to fit any neck size. With the top button fastened, measure around the neckband of the shirt the tie will be worn with. Knit the neckband ½" (1.3 cm) longer than this measurement.

You will need

Yarn

 Light

SHOWN: Vintage DK by Sunrise Fiber Co, 100% superwash merino wool, 3.5 oz (100 g)/231 yd (211 m): Summertime, 1 skein

Needles

- Size 3 (3.25 mm) straight or size to obtain gauge

Pins

- Hand sewing needle and thread

Gauge

26 sts and 38 rows = 4" (10 cm) in St st

Take time to check gauge.

Sizes

Finished measurements: 14½" (37 cm) long, 1¼" (3 cm) high neckband, 3" (7.5 cm) high bow

Construction

All pieces are worked back and forth in rows.

Stitch Guide

GARTER STITCH: Knit every st, every row.

PATTERN STITCH: RS rows: K1, p1, knit to last 2 sts, p1, k1.

WS rows: K1, p1, k1, purl to last 3 sts, k1, p1, k1.

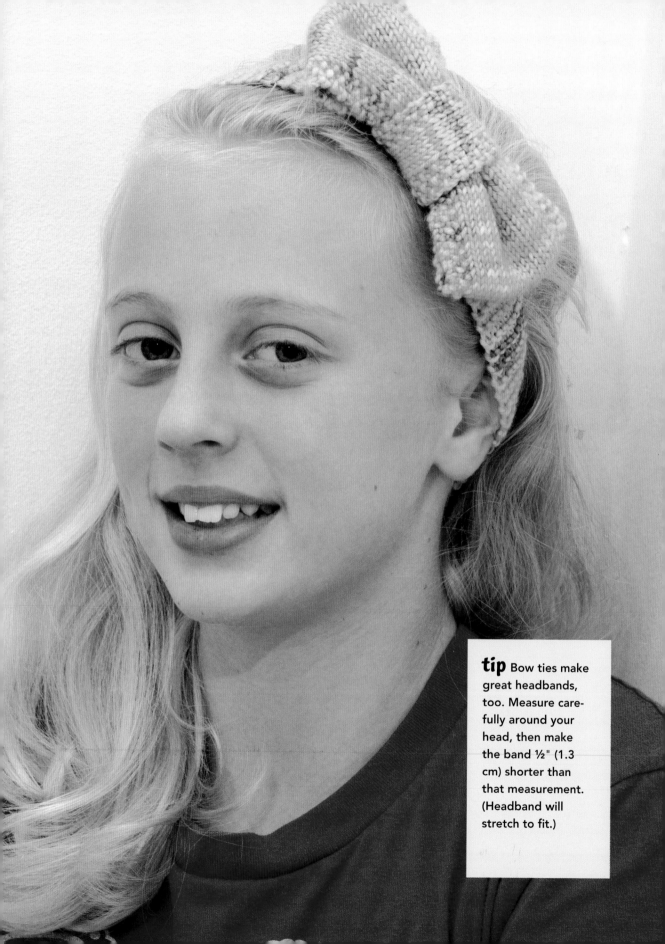

tip Bow ties make great headbands, too. Measure carefully around your head, then make the band ½" (1.3 cm) shorter than that measurement. (Headband will stretch to fit.)

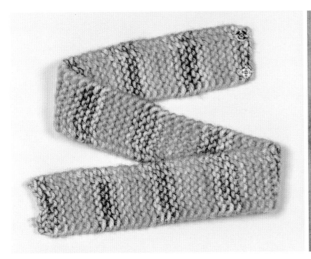
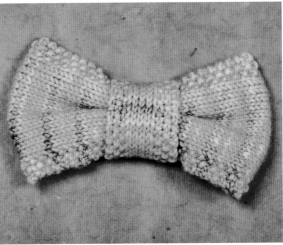

Neckband

CO 8 sts. Work in garter st, slipping first of every row pwise with yarn in back, until piece measures 14½" (37 cm) from CO, or to desired length. BO.

Bow

CO 20 sts. Work in pattern st until piece measures 10" (25.5 cm) from CO, ending with a WS row. BO.

Center

CO 10 sts. Work in pattern st until piece measures 3" (7.5 cm) from CO, ending with a WS row. BO.

Finishing

Weave in ends. Steam all pieces lightly and allow to dry. Overlap ends of neckband ½" (1.3 cm) and mark locations for snaps with pins. Sew snaps to each end of neckband as shown with hand sewing needle and thread.

Fold ends of bow to center with WS tog and sew tog. With seam centered on back of bow, place bow on top of neckband. Wrap center piece around bow and neckband and pin in place. Sew ends of center tog, forming horizontal pleat at center of bow.

| Cast On, page 10 |
| Knit, page 16 |
| Purl, page 18 |
| Bind Off, page 20 |
| Weave Ends, page 49 |
| Blocking, page 52 |
| Snaps, page 61 |

Pencil Roll

This project will help you understand more about gauge. Most of the time in knitting, we match the weight of our yarns to the size of our needles in order to knit fabric that is neither too stiff nor too floppy. But what if we need a tighter or a looser fabric? In this project, the finished fabric needs to be firmer and denser, to keep the pencil points from poking through. To achieve that, we can intentionally choose to knit medium-weight yarn on fine needles. The resulting fabric is thicker and firmer than it would be with bigger needles. The finished piece holds twelve pencils (or pens), plus erasers or other items in the widest slot.

Gauge

26 sts and 36 rows = 4" (10 cm) in St st

Take time to check gauge.

Sizes

Finished measurements: 15" (38 cm) wide, 13" (33 cm) high (7" [18 cm] high when folded)

Construction

Pencil roll is worked in one piece, back and forth in rows.

Stitch Guide

STOCKINETTE STITCH (ST ST): RS rows: Knit. WS rows: Purl.

SEED STITCH: RS rows: *K1, p1; rep from * to end of row. WS rows: *P1, k1; rep from * to end of row.

You will need

Yarn

(4) Medium

SHOWN: Classic Wool Worsted by Patons, 100% wool, 3.5 oz (100 g)/210 yd (192 m): Royal Blue #77132 (MC), 1 skein; Peacock #00218 (CC), 1 skein

Needles

- Size 3 (3.25 mm) straight or size to obtain gauge

Notions

- Tapestry needle

- Hand sewing needle and thread

- Pins

- 1 yd (1 m) of ⅝" (16 mm) ribbon (shown: May Arts EH16 Olive/ Lime)

- **OPTIONAL:** One size 3/0 (¼" [6 mm]) snap

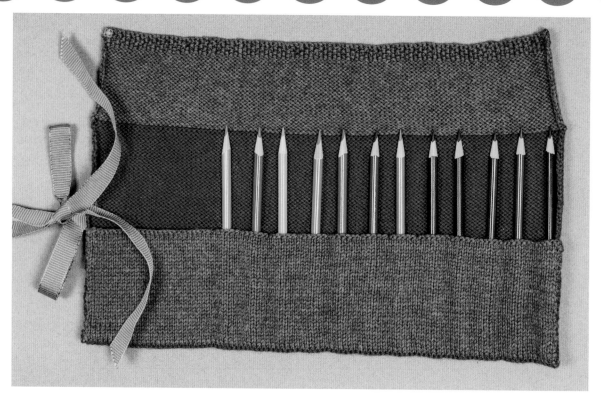

Pencil Roll

Lower Flap

With CC, CO 100 sts. Work in St st until piece measures 3½" (9 cm) from CO, ending with a WS row.

Back

Break yarn and join MC. Purl 1 RS row, forming turning ridge on RS. Work in St st until piece measures 7" (18 cm) from color change, ending with a WS row.

Upper Flap

Break yarn and join CC. Purl 1 RS row, forming turning ridge on RS. Work in St st until flap measures 2¼" (6 cm) from color change, ending with a WS row. Work 4 rows in seed st. BO in patt.

Finishing

Weave in ends and block. Fold lower flap up and pin in place, matching sides. Sew edges tog at both ends (see illustration). Beg at far right, measure 1" (2.5 cm) from edge and mark with a pin. Cont placing pins as shown to mark 12 small slots and one large one. Sew through both layers as shown with matching thread, knotting securely at both ends.

Fold the top flap down and roll from right to left. Fold ribbon about 15" (38 cm) from end and pin in place at left edge of roll. Sew ribbon in place securely.

tip If the left corner of the upper flap sticks out when the roll is closed, add a small snap to secure it (see illustration below).

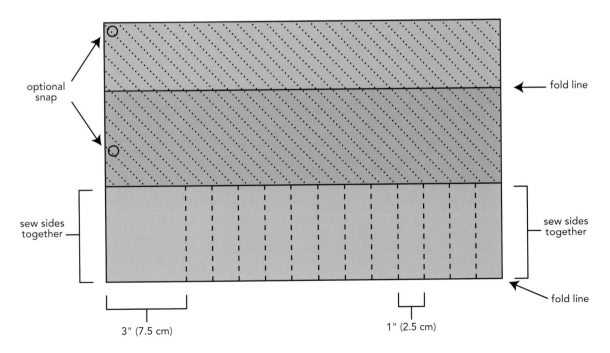

optional snap

fold line

sew sides together

sew sides together

fold line

3" (7.5 cm)

1" (2.5 cm)

Microbes

Real germs are icky, but knitted ones are cute and fun. If you make them for presents, you can say you shared your germs with others!

You will need

Yarn

 Bulky

SHOWN: Wool of the Andes Bulky by Knit Picks, 100% Peruvian Highland wool, 3.5 oz (100 g)/137 yd (125 m): Avocado #25958 (CA), Honey #25956 (CB), Bluebird #25957 (CC), and Crush #25952 (CD), about 30 yd (27 m) each

Needles

- Size 10 (6 mm) straight or size to obtain gauge

Notions

- Wool roving or other stuffing

- Tapestry needle

- Five ⅝" (16 mm) buttons (shown: Slimline #S83)

- Size G/6 (4 mm) crochet hook

Gauge

16 sts and 20 rows = 4" (10 cm) in St st

Take time to check gauge.

Sizes

Finished measurements: About 5" (12.5 cm) high,
7" (18 cm) circumference

Construction

Microbes are worked back and forth in rows.

Stitch Guide

STOCKINETTE STITCH (ST ST): RS rows: Knit.
WS rows: Purl.

Orthomyxovirus (Flu)

With CA and using the long-tail CO method, CO 6 sts. Purl 1 row.

Next row (RS): [K1f&b] 6 times—12 sts.
Purl 1 row.
Next row (RS): [K1f&b] 12 times—24 sts.

Work even in St st until piece measures 4" (10 cm) from last inc row, ending with a WS row.

Next row (RS): [K2tog] 12 times—12 sts.
Purl 1 row.
Next row (RS): [K2tog] 6 times—6 sts.

Break yarn, leaving a 12" (30.5 cm) tail and thread tail through tapestry needle. Thread yarn through rem 6 sts and pull snugly to gather. Without breaking yarn, sew seam with mattress st to about halfway up. Stuff lower half of microbe loosely. Cont sewing seam, adding stuffing as you go. At end of seam, run tapestry needle under 6 CO loops, pulling snugly to gather. Fasten securely and pull yarn tail to inside of microbe.

Shigella (Stomachache)

With CB, work as for Flu.

tip Love knitting microbes? Look for pictures of others you can copy, and don't forget to learn their names!

Finishing

Orthomyxovirus (Flu)

Sew button to center of microbe as shown.

Shigella (Stomachache)

Cut 20 pieces of CD, each about 8" (20.5 cm) long. Fold a strand in half and, using a crochet hook, pull the doubled strand through one knitted st of the microbe, taking care not to pull out any stuffing with the hook. Pull the doubled strand about halfway through and tie in a knot. Cut loop open. Rep with rem strands, spacing them about 1" (2.5 cm) apart, all the way around the microbe's perimeter. Sew 2 buttons in place as shown.

Staphylococcus (Rash)

Arrange 3 globules in triangle formation on a table. Sew tog where globules touch at sides. Sew one globule to top of triangle. Flip microbe over and sew rem globule to bottom of triangle. Sew 2 buttons in place as shown.

Staphylococcus (Rash)

Globules (make 5)

With CC and using the long-tail CO method, CO 4 sts. Purl 1 row.

Next row (RS): [K1f&b] 4 times—8 sts.
Purl 1 row.

Next row (RS): [K1f&b] 8 times—16 sts.
Purl 1 row. Work 8 rows in St st, ending with a WS row.

Next row (RS): [K2tog] 8 times—8 sts.
Purl 1 row.
Next row (RS): [K2tog] 4 times—4 sts.

Break yarn, leaving a 12" (30.5 cm) tail and thread tail through tapestry needle. Thread yarn through rem 4 sts and pull snugly to gather. Without breaking yarn, sew seam with mattress st to about halfway up. Stuff lower half of globule loosely. Cont sewing seam, adding stuffing as you go. At end of seam, run tapestry needle under 4 CO loops, pulling snugly to gather. Fasten securely and pull yarn tail to inside of globule.

Cast On, page 10
Knit, page 16
Purl, page 18
Increases, page 25
Decreases, page 26
Mattress Stitch, page 46
Buttons, page 61

Sweater

Sometimes new knitters worry that making an entire sweater will be difficult. The truth is that once you have mastered basic skills by practicing on smaller items, completing a whole garment is no more challenging. The only difference is that garments take more time to complete because there is more knitted fabric in them. Just relax and enjoy the process, and before you know it you'll be wearing your very own creation!

This sweater is one of the easiest styles to knit. The lower part is worked in the round, then a few stitches are bound off at either side to shape the armholes, then the front and back are worked one at a time, back and forth in rows. The shoulder seams are then joined, and sleeves are knitted flat, from cuff to shoulder. After sewing the underarm seam on each, the sleeves are sewn into the armholes, all with mattress stitch. The only finishing is to work a few rounds of ribbing at the neckline, and weave in the ends.

Gauge

20 sts and 27 rnds = 4" (10 cm) in St st on larger needle

Take time to check gauge.

Sizes

Finished chest measurements: 30 (32, 34, 36, 38, 40, 42, 44)" (76 [81.5, 86.5, 91.5, 96.5, 101.5, 106.5, 112] cm)

Note: Size shown is 36" (91.5 cm).

Stitch Guide

STOCKINETTE STITCH (ST ST): In rnds: Knit every st, every rnd.

In rows: RS rows: Knit. WS rows: Purl.

K1, P1 RIB: In rnds: *K1, p1; rep from * to end of rnd, every rnd.

In rows: RS rows: *K1, p1; rep from * to last st, k1.

WS rows: *P1, k1; rep from * to last st, p1.

You will need

Yarn

4 Medium

SHOWN: Longwood by Cascade Yarns, 100% superwash extrafine merino wool, 3.5 oz (100 g)/191 yd (175 m): Deep Ocean #19, 5 (5, 6, 6, 7, 8, 8, 9) skeins

Needles

- Size 7 (4.5 mm) 16" (40 cm) and 24" (60 cm) circular

- Size 8 (5 mm) 24" (60 cm) circular or size to obtain gauge

Notions

- Stitch marker

- Stitch holders

- Tapestry needle

Sweater

Lower Band

With smaller needle, CO 150 (160, 170, 180, 190, 200, 210, 220) sts. Pm and join for working in rnds, being careful not to twist. Work in k1, p1 rib until piece measures 2" (5 cm) from CO.

Body

With larger needle, knit every rnd until piece measures 11 (12, 13, 13½, 13½, 14, 14, 14½)" (28 [30.5, 33, 34.5, 34.5, 35.5, 35.5, 37] cm) from CO.

Armholes

Next rnd: K70 (75, 79, 84, 87, 92, 95, 100), BO 10 (10, 12, 12, 16, 16, 20, 20) sts, k65 (70, 73, 78, 79, 84, 85, 90), BO 10 (10, 12, 12, 16, 16, 20, 20) sts.

Place last 65 (70, 73, 78, 79, 84, 85, 90) live sts (between armholes) on holder for sweater front.

Back

Working back and forth in rows on back only, work even in St st until piece measures 7½ (8, 8½, 9, 9½, 10, 10½, 11)" (19 [20.5, 21.5, 23, 24, 25.5, 26.5, 28] cm) from underarm BO, ending with a WS row. Break yarn and place live sts on holders as follows: Left shoulder: 19 (21, 22, 23, 23, 25, 25, 27) sts, back neck: 27 (28, 29, 32, 33, 34, 35, 36) sts, right shoulder: 19 (21, 22, 23, 23, 25, 25, 27) sts.

Front

Place held front sts onto larger needle. Rejoin yarn and work back and forth in St st until piece measures 5 (5½, 6, 6½, 6½, 7, 7½, 8)" (12.5 [14, 15, 16.5, 16.5, 18, 19, 20.5] cm) from underarm BO, ending with a WS row.

tip Which size should you make? Measure around the widest part of the wearer's chest with a measuring tape (get help if you're knitting for yourself). Choose the size with a finished measurement 1–2" (2.5–5 cm) larger than your chest measurement, to allow room for movement. This extra space between the body and the sweater is referred to as "ease."

Shape Right Neckline

Next row (RS): K24 (26, 27, 29, 30, 32, 32, 34) and place these sts on holder for left front, k17 (18, 19, 20, 19, 20, 21, 22) and place these sts on holder for front neck, k24 (26, 27, 29, 30, 32, 32, 34).

Cont working on right front as follows: Purl 1 row.
Dec row (RS): K2, ssk, knit to end of row—1 st dec'd.
Next row (WS): Purl.

Rep last 2 rows 4 (4, 4, 5, 6, 6, 6, 6) more times—19 (21, 22, 23, 23, 25, 25, 27) sts. Work even in St st until piece measures 7½ (8, 8½, 9, 9½ 10, 10½, 11)" (19 [20.5, 21.5, 23, 24, 25.5, 26.5, 28] cm) from armhole BO. Place live sts on holder.

Shape Left Neckline

Leaving center 17 (18, 19, 20, 19, 20, 21, 22) sts on holder, cont working on left front as follows: Place 24 (26, 27, 29, 30, 32, 32, 34) held sts on larger needle. With WS facing, rejoin working yarn and purl 1 row.

Dec row (RS): Knit to last 4 sts, k2tog, k2—1 st dec'd.

Next row (WS): Purl.

Rep last 2 rows 4 (4, 4, 5, 6, 6, 6, 6) more times—19 (21, 22, 23, 23, 25, 25, 27) sts. Work even in St st until piece measures 7½ (8, 8½, 9, 9½ 10, 10½, 11)" (19 [20.5, 21.5, 23, 24, 25.5, 26.5, 28] cm) from armhole BO. Place live sts on holder.

Sleeves (make 2)

With smaller needle, CO 37 (39, 41, 47, 47, 51, 51, 51) sts. Work in k1, p1 rib until piece measures 2" (5 cm) from CO, ending with a WS row. With larger needle, work back and forth in St st as follows:

Inc row (RS): K1, k1f&b, knit to last 3 sts, k1f&b, k2—2 sts inc'd.

Rep inc row every 4th row 16 (15, 17, 11, 15, 17, 20, 28) more times—71 (71, 77, 71, 79, 87, 93, 109) sts. Rep inc row every 6th row 3 (5, 5, 10, 8, 7, 6, 1) times—77 (81, 87, 91, 95, 101, 105, 111) sts. Work 5 rows even, ending with a WS row. BO.

Finishing

Weave in ends. Soak pieces in lukewarm water for at least half an hour, then block to measurements. Place left front and back shoulder sts onto smaller needles. With larger needle and RS tog, join shoulder using three-needle BO. Rep for right shoulder.

Neck Edge

With RS facing and smaller 16" (40 cm) needle, beg at left shoulder, pick up and knit 14 (14, 16, 16, 18, 18, 20, 20) sts along left front neck edge to holder, move 17 (18, 19, 20, 19, 20, 21, 22) held center front sts to spare dpn and knit, pick up and knit 14 (14, 16, 16, 18, 18, 20, 20) sts along right front neck to shoulder, move 27

(28, 29, 32, 33, 34, 35, 36) held back neck sts to spare dpn and knit—72 (74, 80, 84, 88, 90, 96, 98) sts. Pm and join for working in rnds. Work k1, p1 rib until edging measures 1" (2.5 cm) from beg. BO loosely.

Sleeves

Sew underarm seams in sleeves, and sleeves into armholes, using mattress st. Weave in ends and steam seams lightly, if needed, to block.

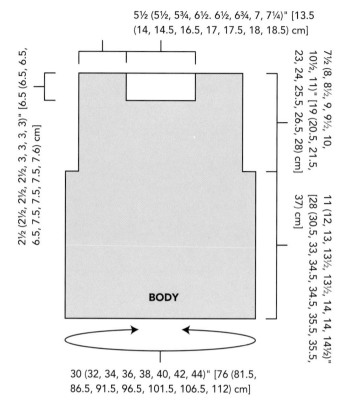

3¾ (4¼, 4½, 4½, 4½, 5, 5, 5½)" [9.5 (10.5, 11, 11.5, 11,5, 12.5, 12.5, 13.5) cm]

5½ (5½, 5¾, 6½. 6½, 6¾, 7, 7¼)" [13.5 (14, 14.5, 16.5, 17, 17.5, 18, 18.5) cm]

2½ (2½, 2½, 2½, 3, 3, 3, 3)" [6.5 (6.5, 6.5, 6.5, 6.5, 7.5, 7.5, 7) cm]

7½ (8, 8½, 9, 9½, 10, 10½, 11)" [19 (20.5, 21.5, 23, 24, 25.5, 26.5, 28) cm]

11 (12, 13, 13½, 13½, 14, 14, 14½)" [28 (30.5, 33, 34.5, 34.5, 35.5, 35.5, 37) cm]

BODY

30 (32, 34, 36, 38, 40, 42, 44)" [76 (81.5, 86.5, 91.5, 96.5, 101.5, 106.5, 112) cm]

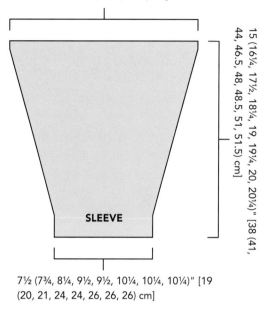

15½ (16¼, 17½, 18¼, 19, 20¼, 21, 22¼)" [39 (41, 44, 46, 48.5, 51.5, 53.5, 56.5) cm]

15 (16¼, 17½, 18¼, 19, 19¼, 20, 20¼)" [38 (41, 44, 46.5, 48, 48.5, 51, 51.5) cm]

SLEEVE

7½ (7¾, 8¼, 9½, 9½, 10¼, 10¼, 10¼)" [19 (20, 21, 24, 24, 26, 26, 26) cm]

tip Be sure to bind off the neck edge loosely so the neckline will stretch enough to go over the wearer's head. Using a needle two or three sizes larger (than the one used for the edging) for the bind off will help keep it loose.

Cast On, page 10
Join a Round, page 29
Knit, page 16
Purl, page 18
Increases, page 25
Decreases, page 26
Bind Off, page 20
Weave Ends, page 49
Three-Needle Bind Off, page 47
Blocking, page 52
Pick Up and Knit, page 49
Mattress Stitch, page 46

Tools and Resources

In addition to knitting needles and yarn, you'll need a few things on hand to measure, mark, and create your knitting. None is very expensive, and most can be found at your local yarn, craft, or fabric store, or from online retailers. Some of these things may already be in your home, so have a look around. Also listed are a few things that aren't essential at first, but that you might like to add to your collection later.

Measuring Tools

Fiberglass tape measure: For measuring bodies, not knitting. It's flexible to bend around heads, chests, etc.

Retractable tape measure: A miniature one from the hardware store, with a metal tape that has a hook on the end. For measuring knitting.

6" (13 cm) metal or plastic ruler: One with nice sharp edges and clear markings, for measuring gauge accurately.

Calculator: A small one that fits into your tool bag.

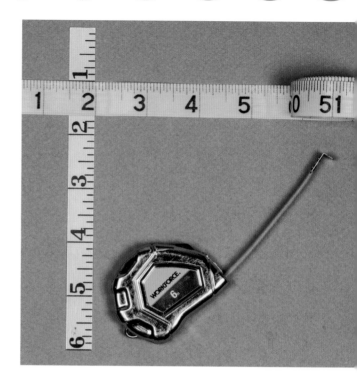

Sewing Tools

Pins and needles: For marking gauge swatches and sewing on embellishments and closures.

Safety pins: For emergency stitch markers and holders.

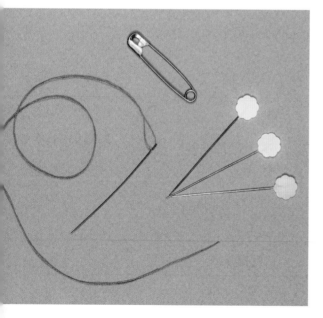

Knitting Tools

Stitch markers: Both opening and closed styles, for keeping track of rows and rounds.

Tapestry needles: Both bent- and straight-tip styles, with large eyes and blunt tips, for seaming knitted pieces and weaving in ends.

Crochet hook: For retrieving dropped stitches and fixing mistakes.

Needle size gauge: Handy for checking the sizes of unmarked needles.

Small, sharp sewing scissors: Better if they have a sheath to cover their blades.

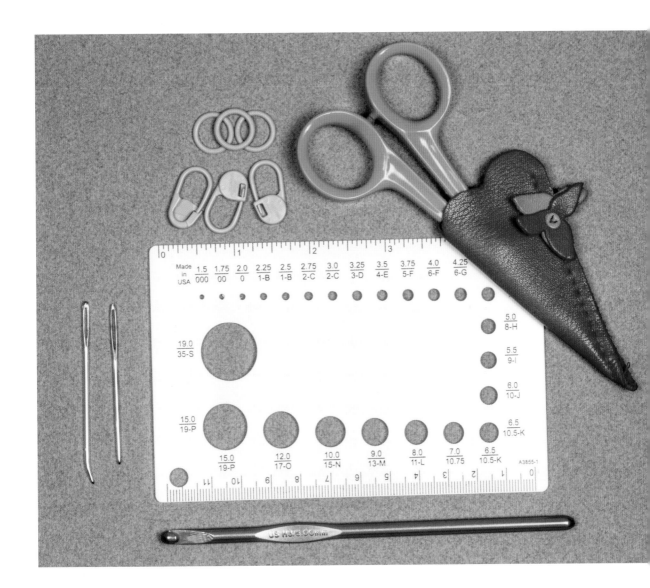

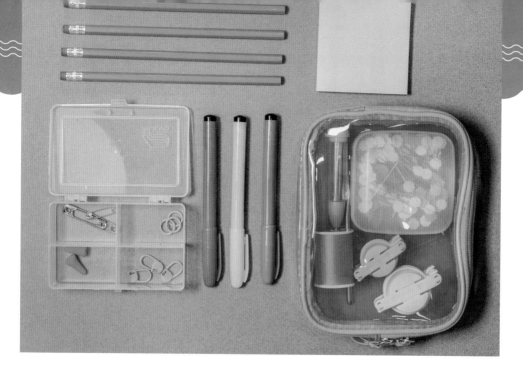

Miscellaneous Tools

Needle point protectors: To keep your knitting from slipping off the needles when you carry it around.

Sticky notes and pencil: For making notes and keeping track of your place in pattern instructions.

Highlighter pen: For marking your size in pattern instructions.

Tool bag or box: Not too big; just large enough to hold all your little tools together. A clear one with a zipper keeps everything secure while allowing you to see what's inside.

Project bag(s): Tote bags, backpacks, even plastic food storage bags are nice for keeping your projects together. Knitters often have more than one project going at a time, so keeping them in separate holders will help keep things organized.

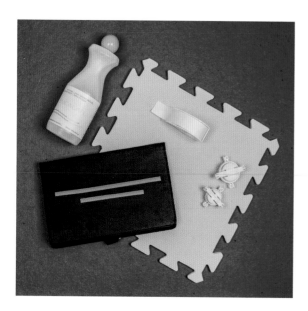

Not Essential, but Nice to Have

Blocking mat: Roll-up or interlocking squares for blocking your knitting

Pompom makers: For making multiple identical pompoms quickly.

Woolwash: Soap made especially for blocking and caring for handknits. Some types do not require rinsing.

Chart/pattern holder: Holds your charts and patterns and marks your place.

Highlighter tape: Helps you keep track of your place in the chart or instructions.

Your Body

The most important tool you have! Take care of it when you knit, by remembering to take breaks and stand up and stretch. Knitting injuries can actually happen, usually from losing track of time and working too long without a break. Take care of yourself by having these things available:

Bright light: Don't work in poor light. It's hard on your eyes, and it causes knitting mistakes.

Comfy chair: Sit up straight, and make sure your back is adequately supported.

Clock or timer: Make sure you take breaks every 20 to 30 minutes, to stand up, stretch, and breathe.

Organization: Keep your tools safely stored at all times. Scissors, pins, and needles of all kinds are for poking into knitting, not people! Protect yourself and the people you live with: make it a rule never to leave your knitting on any seating surface or floor.

Your Knitting Community

Knitting is a group activity! One of the best things about being a knitter is meeting other people who share your interest. Knitters are everywhere, and they love to connect with one another. Here are just a few places where knitters find each other.

Local Yarn Shops

Most towns and cities have yarn stores. Yarn stores are unique in the world of retailing because they are staffed by knitters, who are happy to answer your questions and help you with projects. They often host weekly gatherings where knitters are welcomed into the store to knit together. These gatherings are usually free of charge, and are a great way to meet new friends and get help as you learn. Yarn stores also have classes available, where, for various fees, you can make specific projects, learn particular techniques, or even work with visiting knitting designers and authors. The most vibrant knitting stores are centers of their communities, functioning as gathering places, learning centers, and event coordinators. When you find a yarn store you like, support it with your presence and your dollars; you'll gain more than skills—you'll gain friendships, too.

Knitting Guilds

Guilds are clubs for knitters, and they are always looking for new members of all ages and experience levels. Look in phone directories, check online, or ask at your favorite yarn store to find and visit with a guild. There usually is no charge for non-members to attend their first guild meeting. There you can meet the other members, and learn about their activities. If you decide to join a guild, you'll pay annual dues, in exchange for which you can attend the meetings and take part in guild activities. Some local yarn stores even offer discounts to guild members. Hosting everything from charity knitting to local community events, knitting guilds are great places to meet new friends, learn from experienced knitters, and be a part of the vibrant culture of knitting.

Library, Church, or Volunteer Groups

Many community centers host knitting groups that meet to knit together, share information, and participate in group events. Ask at organizations you already may be a part of whether there are any members who knit. If not, maybe you can start your own new group!

State, County, and Neighborhood Fairs

In the United States, fairs have long been wonderful venues for exhibiting knitted items, and even competing for prizes. Visit the fiber arts exhibits at your local fairgrounds to see what your neighbor knitters have made, and learn how you can enter the competition.

Sheep and Wool Gatherings

Sheep farmers, fiber processors, and independent fiber arts retailers gather annually at fairgrounds to share, compete, and celebrate all aspects of the fiber arts. Knitters, spinners, weavers, and fiber artists of every stripe visit these gatherings. Usually sheep and wool gatherings include livestock and fiber competitions, sheep-to-shawl events (where teams of fiber artists race to see who can finish a knitted shawl from a newly shorn fleece), workshops, and retail areas. These gatherings are the best place to learn where yarn comes from and meet the people who bring it to you. Check with your yarn store, local fairgrounds, and online to learn where a gathering will be near you.

Knitting Events

Conferences, retreats, and other knitting events are held all over the world. They can be as large as the events hosted by Stitches, Vogue, and Interweave, or as small and intimate as a retreat held by your church knitting group. They can be held at hotels, conference centers, or retreat areas. Knitting events often take place over the course of a long weekend. Participants stay together at the venue, attend classes with professional instructors, and take part in events and special presentations held for their enjoyment. Some knitters like to attend the same events every year, where they can connect with knitting friends who come from all over to enjoy the experience together. Knitting events can be just like summer camp for knitters.

Virtual Knitting

The Internet has become a great place for knitters to connect on a daily basis. Social networking sites such as Ravelry offer patterns, tutorials, groups, and events, all from the comfort of your own home computer. In the world of Internet knitting, you can share photos of your work, organize your projects, make virtual friends, and even post your very own patterns for sale. You can connect with knitting designers and authors, and get help from other experienced knitters. Video channels like YouTube are also great resources for knitters. Watching a video can be great when you need help understanding knitting techniques. While not a replacement for hands-on instruction with a teacher or friend, a good video can be really useful when you just need a quick demonstration. If you like learning at your own pace online, try out knitting classes from companies such as Craftsy. For a fee, you'll have access to both class materials (video demonstrations and patterns) and online support for questions you may have. Knitting designers, teachers, and authors often have their own websites, where they post free tutorials, information about events, and blogs about knitting. Clara Parkes (www.knittersreview.com), Carson Demers (www.ergoiknit.com), Stephanie Pearl-McPhee (www.yarnharlot.ca), and even the author of this book (www.maryscotthuff.com) are all knitting professionals whose websites strive to be useful and entertaining.

All of these resources are open and available to knitters of every age and background. You'll enjoy knitting more, and increase your skills when you join in the fun by connecting with your knitting community.

Resources

Cascade Yarns
1224 Andover Park E
Tukwila, WA 98188
www.cascadeyarns.com

Knit Picks
13118 NE 4th Street
Vancouver, WA 97684
www.knitpicks.com

Malabrigo Yarn
Montevideo, Uruguay
www.malabrigoyarn.com

Patons Yarns
320 Livingstone Avenue
South, Box 40
Listowel, ON
Canada
N4W 3H3
www.yarnspirations.com/patons

Sunrise Fiber Company
www.sunrisefiberco.com

About the Author

Mary Scott Huff lives in Fairview, Oregon, and teaches knitting all over the United States. Mary designs knitwear, writes books, blogs, and generally pursues a yarn-centered existence, in a little red house shared with her husband, two children, and two Scottish terriers.

Join Mary in her adventures playing with string at www.maryscotthuff.com.

Acknowledgments

Thank you to my family, for reminding me how to see knitting through brand-new eyes. Phillip, for gamely jumping in to help make needles, and for cheering me on to the finish line. Campbell, for your bottomless well of fantastic design ideas. Lindsay, for knitting for me when I broke my finger. Paisley and Bailey, for wearing dog sweaters in August. I love you all more than is probably reasonable.

Thank you to my friends, Carson and KT; you are living proof that the best part of knitting is knitters.

Thank you to Karen, who always manages to make sense of me. Thank you to the Lindas; both Roghaar and Neubauer, for encouragement and support through my frenetic and fractured adventures.

And thank you to my students: you are my best teachers.

Abbreviations

[ ] work instructions between brackets as many times as directed

* repeat instructions following the asterisk as indicated

" inches

approx approximately

beg begin(ning)

BO bind off

CA color A

CB color B

CC color C or contrasting color

cm centimeter(s)

CO cast on

cont continue

dec decrease(s)(ing)

dpn double-pointed needle(s)

foll following

g gram

inc increase(s)(ing)

k knit

kwise knitwise

k2tog knit two stitches together

LH left hand

m meter(s)

MC main color

oz ounce(s)

p purl

patt(s) pattern(s)

pm place marker

prev previous

pwise purlwise

rem remain(s)(ing)

rep repeat(s)

RH right hand

rnd(s) round(s)

RS right side

sl slip

ssk [slip one stitch knitwise] two times, work these two stitches together through the back loops

st(s) stitch(es)

St st stockinette stitch

tog together

WS wrong side

yd(s) yard(s)

yo yarn over

Index

DON'T MISS THE OTHER BOOKS IN THE SERIES!